BE ANXIETY FREE...
NOW!

THE ULTIMATE GUIDE TO RIDDING YOURSELF OF ANXIETY FOR GOOD

DISCLAIMER

The information provided in this book is designed to provide helpful information on the subjects discussed. This book is not meant to be used, nor should it be used, to diagnose or treat any medical condition. For diagnosis or treatment of any medical problem, consult your own physician. The publisher and author are not responsible for any specific health or allergy needs that may require medical supervision and are not liable for any damages or negative consequences from any treatment, action, application or preparation, to any person reading or following the information in this book. References are provided for informational purposes only and do not constitute endorsement of any websites or other sources. Readers should be aware that the websites listed in this book may change.

Published by Global Health Concerns, LLC

PO Box 10572, Lynchburg, VA 24506

ISBN: 978-1-7373044-0-1

To obtain the complete "Be Anxiety Free…
Now!" program, visit the website at:
www.beanxietyfreenow.com .

BE ANXIETY FREE...
NOW!

Don't Live With Anxiety, Get Rid Of It!

THE ULTIMATE GUIDE TO RIDDING YOURSELF OF ANXIETY FOR GOOD

By Wayne Kelly C.C.Ht.

INTRODUCTION 9

MY STORY...17

WHAT CAUSES ANXIETY 37

HOW TO REDUCE OR GET RID OF ANXIETY 51

NUTRITION & HEALTH... THIS MATTERS MORE THAN YOU
CAN IMAGINE! 61

THE IMPORTANCE OF QUALITY SLEEP 109

YOUR MIND: THERE'S A LOT GOING ON IN THERE! 119

EXERCISE AND NATURE 149

OUTSIDE INFLUENCES 161

RELEASING TRAPPED EMOTIONS 173

CONCLUSION 179

INTRODUCTION

If you are reading this book (which obviously you are) you probably have anxiety and/or depression. You therefore know firsthand how horrible it feels and how much it sucks. I know what you are feeling because I had severe anxiety and mild depression for most of my life. I know that anxiety and depression are all-consuming, it's first and foremost in your thoughts. It rules your life.

Anxiety affects more people now than at any other time in recent history. I believe it has become a worldwide epidemic.

I spent many years figuring out how to get rid of my anxiety and depression, more than 20 years, and I was finally successful. No more daily anxiety and no more depression as a result of my anxiety. I was finally free! I then determined that since I had figured out how to "break the anxiety code", that it was now my goal in life to share this information with the world and help as many people as I could.

You've more than likely already tried different ways of dealing with or trying to get rid of your anxiety. Perhaps you've gone on the internet and read articles, checked out some blogs, and maybe even joined an online group on the subject of anxiety. There's a good chance that you have read other books and tried other programs already in an effort to deal with your anxiety. You may have even seen a therapist or psychiatrist for your anxiety, and maybe you've even been prescribed medication for it.

If you have done any number of these things I applaud you because it shows that you have taken the initiative to understand your anxiety better in an effort to deal with it, and to get rid of it. But I also know that since you are reading this book, that all of the things that you have already tried haven't worked, or they haven't gotten you to the point where you no longer have daily anxiety. It's still a problem for you.

When I was still experiencing my most severe anxiety not that many years ago there were no programs on how to get rid of your anxiety. I know because I desperately looked for them, I wanted to find them, but they didn't exist. There were some books on how to deal with your anxiety, but at that time there really weren't many of them and the ones that I read didn't help that much. I realize that at the time of my writing this book that there are now some anti-anxiety programs available and there are more books on the subject than ever before. I haven't participated in any of these new programs or read many of the newer books because I have already gotten rid of my anxiety using all of the methods and information that I am now about to share with you in this book and program.

So I would like to say one thing here that you probably haven't read or heard before. If you read this book all the way through and follow all of the advice contained in it, and you also listen to the therapeutic recordings that are part of the full program… **you will completely get rid of or drastically reduce your anxiety.**

This won't happen in a matter of years or even months, you will be able to feel relief from your anxiety quickly, and can be free from it in a short time afterwards. I virtually guaranty it.

Following the advice in this book alone may do it for you. But this book works much better as a companion to the entire program. Again, I guaranty that if you combine the information in this book with the therapeutic recordings that are part of the full program, **you will completely get rid of or drastically reduce your anxiety.**

I need to say this though, if you are a person who has been diagnosed with another issue such as bi-polar disorder, schizophrenia or other potentially serious disorder... this book and program will still help you but I cannot guaranty the same complete and absolute results. I would suggest that anyone already diagnosed with a potentially serious disorder first check with your health practitioner before starting this program.

Before we dive into all the information that will actually deal with and then get rid of your anxiety, I would like to say one more thing. This book has been written to be easy to read and understand. I wanted to make sure that anyone who reads this will get all of the benefits of the information contained in it. I refrain from using a lot of technical jargon purposely because I want this information to be easily understood by absolutely everyone. This is not like a technical medical book... rather, this is more of an easy to read instruction manual explaining why you have the anxiety that you have and how you go about getting rid of it. I've kept things pretty simple so that everyone will be able to read this book cover-to-cover over a relatively short period of time.

So, let's get to it.

Chapter 1

MY STORY

I think it's important for me to tell you a little about myself and my anxiety story. I know that whenever I have bought a book or program about any subject, I like to read the author's story about their experience prior to writing their book or developing their program. It's always interesting to know what happened to them, what their experience was, and what motivated them to do what they did. It's also interesting to know that the person may have had similar experiences to myself. So, here is my anxiety story (I promise I won't make it too long).

I was a pretty outgoing kid when I was around the age of 4. Well, I was outgoing around other kids, adults not as much. The age of 4 is about as far back as I can remember, so maybe I was even outgoing with other kids before that... who knows? With other kids I loved being the center of attention and found that I had a knack for making them laugh. So I naturally became kind of a 4 year old comedian around them. I also remember already liking girls. I even invented a game where I got to kiss the girls on the cheeks in nursery school!

My burgeoning comedian career was in full swing at the age of 6 when I entered first grade. I actually remember some of the things that I did to make the other kids laugh, such as telling jokes and dancing on top of my desk whenever the teacher would leave the room. I also remember chatting up the girls in my class... seems I was an early bloomer. Life seemed pretty good and the future bright. But unknown to me, the teacher didn't share my enthusiasm for comedy or elementary school flirting.

Thus, when my first report card was given to my parents everything came crashing down.

I am sure that you remember getting those report cards in elementary school. They had something like ten categories that a kid would be graded on, with room for notes from the teacher. The categories ranged from "spelling" to "art", and everything in between. Well, one of those categories was "behavior", and apparently it was the biggie compared to everything else. I didn't know it, but my teacher had given me the elementary school equivalent of a big fat "F" for

FAIL. Yep, apparently my comedy and affection for chatting with the girls was not a hit with the teacher. Quite the contrary, she must have seen me as a menace to society. The teacher even wrote notes in regards to my "behavior", stating that making the other kids laugh and always talking to the girls was too distracting in the classroom and that it was affecting the other children... and that it needed to be taken care of.

I don't really remember my mother being too mad at this, other than having a kid get a "fail" in behavior being kind of embarrassing to her (hey, it was 1971 and things like this were embarrassing to parents, unfortunately). Making other kids laugh and chatting with the girls wasn't really something that would offend my mother in general I suppose.

Oh, but my father, now that was different story. That "fail" in behavior must have been such an embarrassment for him. I never got a chance to find out how the comedy and chatting with the girls somehow made him seethe with anger, but my guess is that it was the shame and embarrassment he felt because he somehow thought that the teacher must think he was a terrible parent. Maybe my father thought that all the other kid's parents would somehow know that his son got a "fail" in "behavior" and that was just too embarrassing for him to handle, I have no idea. All I know is that the wrath of my father came crashing down on me for that "fail". I don't clearly remember everything that he did, my subconscious mind still has that memory buried deep inside. I do remember that he became extremely angry, and that he did a lot of yelling, and that he beat me too, but I don't remember it all clearly. Whatever he did… it changed me. It was a traumatic enough event that I didn't want it to happen again, it changed me inside, it changed my thinking.

From that day forward I was a different kid in school. No longer was I the class comedian, no longer did I talk with the girls, no longer was I as outgoing as I used to be. Being outgoing, being funny, being me… meant getting an "F" in behavior, it meant I was being bad.

I didn't know it at the time, but I had actually begun to develop anxiety as a result of my experience. My father, who would get angry at just about everything, continued to reinforce the programming that he had been giving to my mind through his angry messages and spankings. By the way, looking back I do believe that my father also suffered from emotional issues such as anxiety and depression, which also caused him to develop an anger management issue.

As the years passed and I advanced through elementary school to junior high school it got worse. Some would say I was just "shy", but that was not the case. Being shy is a form of anxiety, but I was beyond that. I didn't interact with that many kids, I was now very nervous to talk to girls, I became afraid of the teachers and I shrank away from anything that would make me the center of attention usually.

Of course, other kids would take advantage of my anxious personality and would pick on me quite a bit during this time. This just added another layer of anxiety to the mix. By high school I was becoming quite the anxious mess. During this entire time there were many things that had been affecting me and my perceptions of life were being formed. My mind was being "programmed" to think and react in very specific ways as a result of everything that I was experiencing during this time.

I didn't like being the way that I was being, I didn't enjoy the way that I perceived the world around me, I didn't like the way that I reacted to things in life, but I didn't know of any way to change things. At that time I just knew that things were the way that they were, and for me they sucked. Things wouldn't change as I got older, they steadily got worse.

Fast forward about 20 years... and we get to a time when I was thoroughly stressed out regarding just about everything in my life. Everything was causing me stress... my job, my romantic relationship, my finances, my lack of friends... it was causing me much anxiety and I didn't know how to cope. My anxiety had seeped into every aspect of my life to the point that I had extreme social anxiety.

I wouldn't go grocery shopping unless it was late at night, so that I could avoid being around people as much as possible. If I needed gas for my car, I would avoid gas stations that had more than one car already there so as to avoid being around many people. Going out to the movies... forget it, too many people. I didn't enjoy going out to restaurants and bars anymore... too many people. I even started playing hooky from work because I wanted to avoid people. Which was hard to do because I was the manager of a retail store and I had to spend a great deal of time helping customers and working with my employees.

I did attempt to learn how to better cope with my stress and even hoped that I could turn things around, become a more outgoing and happy person. Over the course of a few years, I purchased several self-help books and programs that laid a foundation that would later on become very helpful. Yet at the time, it did nothing to relieve my anxiety other make me feel a bit hopeful that one day I might get some relief.

Then one day it happened... I had my first full blown panic attack. I'm not talking about a garden variety anxiety attack, I had those almost every day, I was a pro at those. I'm talking about the mother-of-all-anxiety-attacks. I was on a plane getting ready to go on a vacation, of all things. I was already anxiety ridden regarding having to fly in a plane, plus the 9/11 attacks had just happened the year before, so I wasn't in a very good place mentally.

Although the stage was already set for a big anxiety attack with everything that I just described, something happened that acted as a trigger for something bigger. I heard several people speaking Arabic on the plane and although I didn't want that to make me think anything bad or be paranoid, it happened anyway. I didn't want to be racist or judgmental and think that just because these people were speaking Arabic that they were terrorists, it happened anyway.

The plane hadn't even left the gate yet and it happened. I was filled with intense fear. The adrenaline was pumping, my heart was racing, and I felt trapped. I thought that I was having a heart attack, I had never felt anything like this before. I can't really begin to describe how intense it felt, but anyone who has ever had a real full-on panic attack already knows. If you have never had one, you will never know that type of fear, and I am truly happy for you if you haven't.

I came very close to getting off the plane, but I somehow managed to do enough self-talk to calm myself down to a standard anxiety attack level. I stayed on the plane, and I am glad that I did because it ended up helping me to deal with both anxiety and panic attacks in the future. I literally self-talked to myself the entire flight from Washington, DC to Florida. The plane didn't blow up and it didn't crash, obviously.

I ended up spending my entire vacation thinking about what had just happened, and thinking about the level of anxiety I had been living with as an adult. I realized that I needed help, and I did what most people do in situations like this. I made an appointment with a psychiatrist and a therapist when I got home from my vacation. This decision that I made turned out to be both a blessing and a curse.

I saw a therapist for ten sessions, which was all my health insurance would cover. Thinking back, I would have benefitted from more therapist sessions and no visit to the psychiatrist. The therapist was great, in that, she gave me a safe place to express myself and talk about the things that I was aware of that were causing me the higher-than-normal levels of anxiety. She allowed me to figure out what I probably needed to do in order to get out of the situations that were fueling this extreme anxiety. Unfortunately, the situations that were causing the extreme anxiety were not ones that could be easily changed or gotten out of quickly.

Then there was the psychiatrist. It was really the psychiatrist that was the blessing and curse combined. He didn't do very much now that I think about it. My first visit was the longest one, yet it was less than an hour long. He asked how I felt, asked what I thought was the cause of the anxiety and the panic attack, asked how it was affecting my daily life and so forth. He stated that going to the therapist was good and that he wanted to see me again after the 10 therapy sessions were over. He suggested that I probably had a chemical imbalance that was causing the extreme anxiety and that the best way to deal with it was to take a prescription drug. Then, he wrote me a prescription for Xanax and told me to take 1 to 2 pills… every single day.

The Xanax seemed like a blessing at first, because after taking that first one I felt, for the first time, a feeling of not caring much about any of the stuff that caused me the anxiety. It was actually good for me to have been able to have something that provided some relief. But, this should never have been a prescription to take 1 or 2 pills of every single day for the rest of my life. This should have been a "take only when you have extreme anxiety or a panic attack" prescription. And so, I became addicted to the Xanax.

Although the Xanax did take the edge off the anxiety, and it allowed me to not care as much about the things that were seemingly causing my anxiety, it also dulled all of my senses. I lived with a perpetual mind fog, I couldn't think clearly and I wanted to sleep all of the time. I would realize later on that this really was not the right way to deal with the anxiety.

A few years later I got married and moved to a different state, and with that came a different psychiatrist. Luckily the new psychiatrist knew that daily dosages of Xanax was bad for me and took me off of it. Unfortunately, he just replaced it with Prozac.

The Prozac didn't really seem to do much for me, leading me to understand that my anxiety was not an abnormal "chemical imbalance". I started to think that I just didn't know how to deal with stress very well, that it affected me in an extreme way, more so than most people. My thinking was on the right track, but I still didn't really know what to do about it. The self-help books and programs that I had read and listened to a few years back didn't really address anxiety specifically.

Daily life was hard for me… I experienced almost constant anxiety about everything in my life. The move to the new state with the new wife turned out to be a very bad series of decisions. My fresh marriage was turning out to be not very good, we were actually not compatible at all. The city that I was now living in I loathed with every fiber of my being, it just was not the right place for me. My job had gone from being pretty much "okay" to a stress filled circus of anxiety. Things were not going in the direction I had hoped.

After almost 4 years of this, my wife and I separated and we were going through a divorce. As a result, I also become saddled with virtually all of the debt that we had created together. My job had gone from the work of one person to that of what 3 people should have been doing, it was a juggling act that I was barely able to keep up with. I was living in a house that my boss owned in a somewhat unsafe and low-rent district that added to my growing depression. I had no real friends to speak of, other than my sister who lived a few miles away at this point. Things had just seemed to have gotten worse.

I began to self-medicate myself to dull the ever growing anxiety and depression. I started smoking again, close to a pack a day, which I hadn't done in many years. I was drinking alcohol heavily every night, and I even started taking prescription pain pills with the booze to further dull the emotions. I was lucky that I didn't accidentally kill myself with that combination. I would wake up each morning incredibly hung over, having to go to the job that I could barely handle anymore. Then I would come home after work and do it all over again. Things had gotten pretty bad.

Then one day in late September of 2008, due to my ever growing dereliction of my duties at work, I got into some trouble with my boss. I won't go into the details here, they don't really matter. What matters is that I knew that I could very soon lose my job, and I could lose the place where I was living since my boss owned the house I was renting. This began my super-anxiety-filled-freak-out. Yes, I was about to have my second real panic attack.

I began drinking and smoking that evening, which really were things that I shouldn't have been doing at a moment when I needed to be thinking clearly. I discussed the situation with my sister, who came up with a couple of good short-term solutions to what was seemed to be a bad near-term future. She offered to let me and my 2 dogs stay at her house short term, which was very nice of her. But she also made the suggestion to maybe go live with our mother in Virginia for a while, while I figured out what to do next.

After going back to what was still my home at that moment, my mind was racing and that's when the panic attack truly kicked in. I was almost paralyzed with fear. I didn't relish the idea of what the day was going to be like at work in the morning, I really thought it would be a bad scene and that I would be losing not only my job but my place to live. I had no idea what to do.

Then I remembered the suggestion of my sister, I could go to stay with our mother in Virginia for a while and get things sorted out. My sister meant to suggest to do this *eventually*, but my fear-soaked brain thought it was a great idea to do *RIGHT NOW*. So that's what I did… I spent the rest of the night deciding what to take with me and what to leave behind. I packed up my essentials and put them all in the car, along with my two dogs. I then wrote a letter of resignation to my boss.

By dawn I was ready to go. I drove over to my office and slipped my resignation letter under the front door and then hit the road. I drove out of that city and watched it slowly disappear in my rearview mirror, as my anxiety slowly started to subside. I realized that this was possibly a very bad idea, but at the moment my panic attack had gone away and I was feeling better. And that's all I really cared about at that moment.

I found a welcoming new home in Virginia with my mom. I was experiencing a "do-over", you know, just like we would say as kids when you screwed up your turn while playing a game, you'd shout "do-over!" and you got to do it over again, to try again. This was my "do-over".

This is when my great education in what anxiety really was and how to get rid of it began. I already had been educating myself in self-help ideologies and learned many great things that would eventually help me figure everything out. But now I was to begin learning more specifically about anxiety and the often resultant depression.

I spent the next 10+ years learning about anxiety: where does it come from, why do we experience it, why do some people experience it more than others, how do we deal with it, why do so many people experience it on a constant basis, and the million dollar question…**how do we get rid of it**?

Weeding out the things that didn't work very well from the things that did, I managed to figure out what was causing myself to have all this severe anxiety. I also managed to figure out that the vast majority of people in the world who also experience severe anxiety have the same general causes for it.

I learned what works well and what does not, and why. I know what works because it worked on me and I know what works on most people because I've seen it work on them too. I've read many books on the subject of anxiety and depression, I've gone through many different programs for them myself, and I have taken numerous courses on the subject, including some to become certified in certain aspects of assisting people with getting rid of their anxiety and anxiety related depression.

My lifetime of anxiety, including 20+ years of overall research, education and training on the subject, has allowed me to discover practices and processes that will drastically relieve or get rid of severe anxiety in virtually anyone who is experiencing it. I pretty much guaranty it.

Today I am free from anxiety, can you believe it? Yes, you can believe it! I am testament to the fact that virtually anyone can overcome their severe anxiety and resultant depression. Whether you have had it your entire life as I did, or it's something that has popped up more recently in your life, you can be free of it for good!

So, let's get started!

Chapter 2

WHAT CAUSES ANXIETY

So, what causes anxiety anyway? Well, a lot of things actually. But let me first explain what anxiety is and why it's not always a bad thing.

Anxiety is a normal response to a threat or perceived threat. It prepares both the mind to be alert and the body to take action in response to the threat or perceived threat. This would have been part of what kept early humans alive in the days of saber-toothed tigers and aggressive tribes that were competing for hunting and gathering areas. Anxiety was helping humans stay alive, and to a certain degree it still does to this very day. Some anxiety is normal, believe it or not.

But anxiety is meant to be beneficial in small doses and only when really needed. The human body and mind can easily handle anxiety when it's needed here and there, it's designed to. But our bodies and minds are not designed to experience anxiety on an ongoing basis. I'll explain further in a moment.

Anxiety isn't just one thing, its many things. What do I mean by that? Anxiety consists of several different experiences all at the same time. If you've ever experienced anxiety, and I know you have, you will recognize the following list of experiences associated with anxiety:

- Emotional – the emotional changes that occur during anxiety can range anywhere from slight nervousness and feeling uneasy, to sheer panic.
- Thought Patterns – thought patterns begin to change that match up with the emotional changes such as fear based thoughts, racing thoughts, confusion and worst-case scenario thinking.
- Physical – going along with the changes in emotion and thinking are physical changes, such as increased heart rate, sweating, tense muscles, shaking, difficulty breathing and swallowing, difficulty speaking and even falling unconscious.

So you see, anxiety is a multi-faceted experience that occurs in both the mind and the body. Now that you have read this you can think about your own experience with anxiety and recognize that there is a lot going on when you are experiencing it.

So getting back to what I wrote a couple of paragraphs ago, our minds and bodies are not designed to experience anxiety on an ongoing basis. The combination of the intense emotional, mental and physical changes occurring in our bodies is too much for it to handle on an ongoing and daily basis. Your body can literally begin to wear out and your mind to wear down. It's like driving a car at 100 mph all day long everyday… the car can handle it okay at first, but over time certain parts begin to quickly wear down and then eventually entire systems begin to fail and things start to quickly fall apart.

I'll give some examples of what is happening inside of your mind and body while experiencing anxiety to give a little better understanding of why it can be destructive over time. Some of the anxiety chemicals and hormones responsible for what you are feeling during anxiety are listed below.

• Norepinephrine – This is responsible for many of the physical effects of anxiety since this is responsible for things like increased energy during fight-or-flight situations. This is responsible in part for the myriad of physical changes such as shaking, sweating, increased heart rate, and difficulty in breathing, swallowing and talking.

Norepinephrine also causes blood vessels to narrow which increases blood pressure. Persistent increased amounts of these effects can cause damage to blood vessels, increase blood pressure, and lead to an increased risk for heart attacks and stroke. They are also known to cause headaches and insomnia, which of course can lead to more serious health complications.

- Epinephrine – This is also known as adrenaline, which I am sure that you have heard of. Epinephrine is very similar in its physical effects to norepinephrine. One of the effects of epinephrine that is different though is that it relaxes muscles in the airways that lead to your lungs. This allows your body to get more oxygen in situations where it might need it… like to run away from something, or to stand and fight it. Persistent increased amounts of epinephrine can lead to virtually all of the same health risks listed for norepinephrine.

- Cortisol – This is your body's main stress hormone and too much of it can lead to the same issues that are listed above. Your hypothalamus and pituitary glands both regulate the amount of cortisol in your body, and it is needed for many beneficial things such as regulating blood pressure, reducing inflammation, managing your body's usage of carbohydrates, proteins and fats, among other wonderful things. It is produced by your adrenal glands and is released in larger amounts during times of stress. It works with epinephrine to assist you in fight-or-flight situations by narrowing the arteries while the latter increases the heart rate. There are a few other things going on when cortisol is pumped into your system during stressful situations but the main thing to know here is that too much cortisol in your system for too long can lead to many health issues such as increased blood sugar levels, digestive problems, suppressed immune system issues and heart disease.

All of the above can also interfere with what I'll refer to as "good mood" chemicals in the brain and body. The "good mood" chemicals are ones that you have probably heard of such as serotonin, dopamine and GABA. What these chemicals do in the body and brain are way beyond the scope of explanation of this book. But they all play a role in our feeling happy, safe and fulfilled. Although there are countless studies ongoing regarding how norepinephrine, epinephrine and cortisol might interfere with the production or uptake of the "good mood" chemicals, the jury is still out on exactly what is going on between them all. I have come to know that some researchers are already stating that excessive amounts of cortisol can interfere with the production of serotonin, it's a rather complicated process but what matters here is that it is further proof that too much stress and anxiety leads to more anxiety.

If you would like to know more about what these "good mood" chemicals do to make you feel so good, I would suggest doing some research online or finding a more comprehensive book on them. Perhaps someday in the not too distant future I will write a book about it, but until then, I'll concentrate on helping people get rid of their anxiety because after all, that's what we really care about here, right?

So all this talk of hormones and chemicals causing our anxiety is nice and informative, but what is causing you to experience anxiety all the time? Why do you experience severe anxiety? What are the underlying reasons this is all happening? *Just why the hell is this happening?* All great questions that I hope to answer now.

There is a lot of talk amongst health practitioners about anxiety and depression being the result of a chemical imbalance in the body or brain. Well, while that's true, most people don't just start having chemical imbalances for no reason. Unfortunately, it seems to me that many health practitioners treat anxiety as if it's something that just popped-up recently and that prescribing pharmaceutical drugs is the way to balance things out again. "Here is your prescription, take this every day for the rest of your life and you might be okay". For most people, that's going to be a very bad way of treating anxiety.

Yes, there are going to be some people who have a physical disorder that creates an imbalance of certain hormones and chemicals in the body that then create anxiety and/or depression. Here are a few examples:

• Severe cases of hyperthyroidism or hypothyroidism can result in noticeable mood changes including anxiety and/or depression. While it's widely believed that approximately 1% of adults in the United States have hyperthyroidism, and another 4% have hypothyroidism, it is not believed to be the cause for people's anxiety in most cases.

- Adrenal gland tumors, or Cushing's Syndrome, can cause anxiety in individuals because it affects the adrenal glands ability to produce cortisol, it effectively causes it to produce too much of it. The odds of having this are pretty rare though, only 1 out of every 500,000 people have this.

- Lyme disease is a bacterial infection that is contracted from the bite of an infected black-legged tick. The bacterial infection causes the person to feel extreme fatigue, which in turn often causes depression. It is thought to also cause anxiety in some people, but to a much lesser extent than the usual extreme fatigue.

- Estrogen fluctuations during menopause can often cause anxiety or depression. This, unfortunately, will affect every woman at some point after the age of 40 usually. But the good news it doesn't have to cause anxiety and depression.

- Certain neurological disorders such as Alzheimer's disease can also cause anxiety.

This is not an exhaustive list, but in all the research that I have done on the subject these were some of the main disorders or diseases that would come up in studies and articles. As you can see, the chances of getting or having any one of these are pretty slim, with the exception of menopause.

So where does that leave us? That's the million dollar question, what is the most likely cause of your anxiety? The million dollar answer, if you will, is **your experiences in life**. It is a combination of personal experiences within our human social systems, combined with our learned perceptions and judgments, that play the biggest roles. But it's more that that still, it is also not having our needs met. That sounds like a lot, doesn't it?

Let me say here and now that it is highly unlikely that there is something wrong with you. The reason that you have severe anxiety, and maybe even depression, is because of a myriad of things that you have experienced throughout your life. Much of it happened when you were a kid learning about the world, some of it has probably been poor choices with things like what you put in your body regarding food and drugs, some of it could be physical or emotional trauma that you've experienced. The list is almost endless. But it's basically, the experiences in your life.

I am going to give you a list of just some of the more common reasons for why people experience anxiety. You'll probably identify with at least a few of them, if not many of them. These are anxiety inducing reasons that I have seen listed in many different books, articles, programs and through my own insight. It is not an exhaustive list yet it covers a lot.

- Being criticized
- Being humiliated
- Being intimidated
- Being told your stupid or worthless
- Being rejected
- Being told you are unattractive
- Experiencing verbal abuse
- Experiencing physical abuse
- Experiencing sexual abuse
- Being bullied
- Feeling extremely shy
- Lack of friends
- Lack of a social life
- Lack of any intimate relationships
- Being in an unfulfilling relationship
- Feeling your life is without meaning or purpose
- Stress in the workplace

- Stress in your home
- Not having enough money
- Financial stress
- Living someplace where you do not want to live
- Living in a crime ridden neighborhood
- Not achieving your goals
- Getting sick/ill
- Becoming physically injured
- Having to spend time in a hospital
- Focusing too much on your past
- Thinking too much about your future
- Changing schools
- Changing jobs
- Moving to a new city
- Moving to a new country
- Getting in trouble with the law
- Too much negative news on TV or the Internet
- Not getting enough sleep
- Poor diet, too much junk food
- Not getting enough minerals and vitamins
- Too much caffeine
- Too much artificial sweeteners
- Smoking cigarettes
- Doing certain drugs

- Overusing certain drugs
- Consuming too much alcohol
- Not getting enough exercise
- Not spending enough time in nature

The list goes on and on, I could easily fill several more pages with reasons why you might be experiencing anxiety or even depression. I am sure that you were able to identify with more than one of the reasons on the list. There is a good chance that you have some reasons that I didn't list as well.

This brings us to the next million dollar question, the one we have all been waiting for... how do I significantly reduce or *get rid of* my anxiety? I will begin to answer that question in the next chapter.

Chapter 3

HOW TO REDUCE OR GET RID OF ANXIETY

The chapter we've all been waiting for, right? I remember when I was experiencing severe anxiety as an adult, the thing I cared most about was getting rid of the feelings that I was experiencing due to my anxiety. I just wanted it to stop, I wanted to feel normal, or at least what I thought normal was supposed to feel like. I was interested in the causes as well, for sure. But as you already know, when you are in the grips of anxiety... especially when its daily and constant anxiety, you mostly just want to find out how to make it stop, or at least make it less extreme.

So how did I get rid of my anxiety?

I got rid of my anxiety slowly, and deliberately, over a period of approximately 10 years. This does not include the time that I was on prescription drugs for it either. My real personal research began after I took myself off of the prescription drugs.

Don't worry, I am not suggesting that it's going to take you ten years to get rid of your anxiety. But it took me that long because I didn't know what was going to work and what wasn't. I had to try many different things, and through trial and error I was able to find what worked the best for me. After finding out what was working the best for me, I started looking into what would work best for everybody else too.

I don't know exactly how much money I spent over that 10 year period of time looking for what would get rid of my anxiety, but it was in the thousands of dollars, easily as much as twenty thousand dollars. You've probably already spent a significant amount in your own search, hopefully not as much as I did. But you can feel good in knowing that you shouldn't have to spend much money after reading this book and participating in my course.

I tried many different things, and I am sure that some of these you have already tried. Some things helped, others didn't. Some things ended up being virtually the same thing as another method or product I tried, while others were unique. Some things were well thought out, others just hap-hazardously thrown together and were a joke.

So what were some of these things that I tried?

Self-Help Books

One of the easiest things to do when looking for help with anxiety or anything related to anxiety, is to find a self-help book. Kind of like this one, right? There are more self-help books out there for anxiety, depression, and general positive thinking than you can shake a stick at. Why anyone would want to shake a stick at them is unknown to me, it's just a stupid old saying. Some of the books have some great advice while others do not, and some of them are just pure crap.

I know that I'll be stepping on some toes of the self-help gurus out there by writing this, but... many of the books out there regarding anxiety, depression and general positive thinking have very nice suggestions but often they don't address the underlying issues causing the anxiety. When they do try to address the underlying causes of anxiety, they don't give realistic advice on how to deal with those underlying causes. Just telling someone to say daily affirmations and thinking positive thoughts is not going to get rid of anybody's anxiety or resultant depression.

I suppose that if you constantly said affirmations and practiced positive thinking (as best you can while experiencing extreme anxiety) throughout the day, every day, for many, many, many years you might get some decent results. Yet, I doubt it. That's because daily affirmations and positive thinking do not go deep enough, they barely scratch the surface of the reasons for having anxiety. Many self-help books are the same suggestions as in other books with a lot of fluff and cheerleading, or they begin to indulge into metaphysical ideas that not everybody is comfortable with. I am a very open minded person to many different ideas and concepts, but not everybody else is and that makes the advice in some books an immediate turn off for some people.

I remember every time I would buy a new self-help book on anxiety, or something along the lines of positive thinking, I would be excited to start learning everything. I would eagerly read the first chapter or two and then would start practicing whatever it was they were telling me to practice. But, as always, the excitement would begin to fade away as I noticed that I wasn't experiencing much in the way of results. Sure, I felt better at first, but that was mainly due to the excitement of the prospect that the book might be the one that actually helps me get rid of the anxiety. I never did find that one book that did it all, unfortunately. I did sometimes get some nuggets of wisdom that helped me along my journey to being anxiety free, but there was never a book that covered all the bases that would free me from it.

Self-Help Programs

Then there were the programs that I had purchased. Quite often it was a combination of a book and some recordings (sounds familiar, doesn't it?). Some of these programs weren't much better than the books that I had been buying, and again some were outright crap. But yet, there were some that really started to help me with the anxiety.

The programs ranged from everything from listening to someone give me affirmations I needed to repeat every day to reciting prayers, from starting a new diet to unique ways of releasing old emotions, from astrological concepts to different types of hypnotherapy.

I participated in more programs than I can remember. I don't clearly remember some of them because many of them were virtually useless. But the ones that had some valuable information and practices, I listened to and participated in multiple times. Some of the things that are part of my program are bits and pieces from those other programs. I've kept the bits that work and thrown out the pieces that do not. I can easily say that my program is not some sort of rip-off of the other programs, because I learned that only bits and pieces of those other programs were useful. Trust me, you would have to purchase and participate in a lot of programs to even get close to what you are getting in my program.

The Stuff That Worked Best

In addition to the bits and pieces from some of the books and programs that were worth remembering was information regarding two main realms that ended up helping me the most.

Surprisingly enough, one of them was the stuff that I was putting in my body. I was finding out that nutrition plays a huge part in how we feel emotionally. I never would have thought that nutrition would affect a person's mind and emotions as much as it does, but it does. We'll be covering this in more detail in another chapter.

Similar to nutrition were drugs... specifically things like caffeine, alcohol and nicotine. Those are the big 3 that most of us consume that can affect our body and mind to a point that it can make anxiety worse. If you are consuming any other drugs, they can also greatly affect your anxiety. We'll also be covering this in more detail in another chapter.

Then there was the biggie, the grand-daddy of them all... the subconscious part of the mind. I learned over years of doing research that the number one reason why so many of us develop and experience anxiety, especially severe anxiety and depression, is because of the stuff that swirls around in our subconscious. Our subconscious mind remembers everything that has ever happened to us, and I do mean *everything*. We don't consciously remember everything because the conscious part of our mind is not designed to... it's designed to deal with what is right in front of us. But believe me, your subconscious remembers it all... the good, the bad and the ugly.

Because this is the biggie, there will be a couple of chapters that cover this in greater detail. I promise though, I won't be boring you with textbook style explanations of it. I will be giving you the interesting stuff, the juicy bits and pieces, and the stuff that will ultimately help you to get rid of your anxiety.

I will say one last thing before I end this chapter. I have mentioned nutrition, drugs and the subconscious mind here because they are the three things that affected me the most when it came to moods, emotions, and my outlook on life. They are the three main things that also affect you and everybody else on the planet, when it comes to mood, emotions and outlook on life. By addressing all three in this book and program, we will be effectively addressing all that needs to be addressed to get rid of your anxiety.

I will say this one more time though, if you are a person who has been diagnosed with another issue such as bi-polar disorder, schizophrenia or another potentially serious disorder... this book and program will still help you, but I cannot guaranty the same absolute results as I do for others. I would suggest that anyone already diagnosed with a potentially serious disorder first check with their health practitioner before starting this program.

And with that, let's begin!

Chapter 4

NUTRITION & HEALTH... THIS MATTERS MORE THAN YOU CAN IMAGINE!

One of the things that I never thought much about while battling my anxiety was nutrition. Little did I know that what we eat and drink (and sometimes smoke) has a lot to do with how we feel not only physically, but also mentally and emotionally. I was fortunate enough to come across some information, while looking for a natural remedy for indigestion, that would forever change the way that I looked at how foods and drinks affects our moods and emotions.

So, back in 2010 I started developing indigestion on a fairly regular basis. I didn't pay it much attention at first, but then it started getting worse. It went from being uncomfortable to being quite painful at times. Since my anxiety was still pretty much in full-on mode at that time I even wondered if maybe I was having a heart attack. Like just about everyone else in the world, I didn't start to worry about it until it caused me pain.

So, after doing some research online I found that one of the best remedies was a glass of water with a teaspoon of apple cider vinegar mixed in it. I tried it and lo-and-behold it really worked! Being so impressed with this natural remedy, I started reading more information from the author of the article online. The author, by the way, was Dr. Edward Group. I downloaded more nutritional information from his website, including remedies for many other common things and an eBook of his called "The Green Body Cleanse" that gave me a ton of good information on how to become healthier in a relatively easy way. I do not know Dr. Group personally, but I would highly recommend that anyone reading this book look up Dr. Group and his organization Global Healing.

I became more interested in nutrition and this led me to finding even more information on how foods, vitamins and minerals, and other consumables affect not only our bodies, but our emotions and moods. Over the coming years I would start reading articles, research studies and books on the subject. I found videos of interviews with the new experts and started watching new documentaries that covered the subject.

I won't go into every story of how I came across all of this information, but it became clear to me that an important part of the anxiety puzzle is what we consume. I was discovering first-hand how reduction/elimination of some items, and the addition of others, was greatly improving the way that I felt in regards to my anxiety.

The human body is an amazingly complicated thing. I cannot even begin to explain or describe many of the processes that occur in our bodies that keep us alive and functioning. Our bodies are also amazingly resilient and can handle experiencing many not-so-nice things. Our bodies know how to fight off both bacterial and viral infection on their own. Our bodies know how to repair themselves from physical injuries. Our bodies even know how to repair and recover from diseases and conditions such as cancer... yes its true.

But whether or not our bodies actually do all of these amazing things depend on whether or not our bodies are getting all of the nutrition they need. There are other factors as well, but nutrition is first and foremost. In our modern cultures and societies it is actually becoming more difficult to achieve proper nutrition. There are many reasons for this, but that's another subject, perhaps for another book.

So, I will now outline the main things that affect us in regards to what we put into our bodies, or don't put into our bodies, that can cause anxiety. I'll explain what you should be avoiding or eliminating, and what you should be including in your daily consumption. Of course, I'll be explaining why you should be either eliminating of including these, because who wants to just be told what they should and shouldn't be doing without good explanation? Not me.

The Bad Things to Avoid or Eliminate

Caffeine:

When it comes to battling anxiety, caffeine is one of your worst enemies. Even people who don't suffer from daily anxiety can experience temporary anxiety from consuming too much caffeine because of what it does to your body and brain. I remember many times in the past when I felt that I needed to drink more than my usual 2 cups of coffee a day to stay awake for some reason… and every time I exceeded those 2 cups I would get an anxiety attack. Luckily in those cases they were temporary and after a few hours I would feel better.

Caffeine not only can give you a temporary anxiety attack, but for those who suffer from anxiety already, caffeine can be a real nightmare. In fact, if you suffer from daily anxiety and you drink caffeinated drinks, whether its coffee, tea or soda, you may be inducing a higher level of anxiety than what you actually have. Just quitting caffeine, or greatly reducing it in your diet, could be all that you need to do! However, for most people reading this book, quitting caffeine probably won't cure you of your anxiety, but it sure will help you a great deal.

Why is caffeine so bad for anxiety? Well, it's basically the fact that it is a stimulant that increases stress hormones. When you consume caffeine, it causes your body to produce cortisol, norepinephrine and epinephrine (adrenaline). As we have already covered in an earlier chapter, all three of these are stress hormones that make you feel anxiety. The more of these that are being released in your body, the more anxiety you feel. We don't want that!

Another reason why caffeine can make your anxiety worse is that it is a diuretic, meaning it makes your body expel liquid, meaning that it makes you pee a lot. When your body is being made to pee a lot you lose a lot of minerals that your body would normally be using. One of those minerals is magnesium. Research has shown that a magnesium deficiency can cause several different problematic issues including poor sleep and anxiety.

Which leads us to the fact that caffeine can affect your sleep. We will be discussing the importance of sleep in a bit more detail in another chapter, but getting enough good quality sleep is extremely important in getting rid of anxiety.

So what to do? If you are like many people you probably drink many things that are caffeinated like coffee, tea and sodas. You really want to decrease the amount of caffeine that you consume each day. If you can, it would be even better to try to quit caffeine altogether. It's not as hard as you may have heard. Whatever it is that you are drinking that has caffeine, just reduce the amount you drink to begin with.

For example, I used to drink 3 cups of coffee every day, sometimes 4 cups. I chose to decrease my caffeine gradually to avoid the dreaded caffeine withdrawal. It was pretty easy... each week I simply reduced my caffeinated coffee amount by 1 cup, and if I still wanted to drink that cup I would drink decaffeinated coffee instead. After 3 weeks I was down to just 1 cup of regular coffee a day. Some days I drank a second cup of decaf coffee, but just because I like the taste of coffee. By the fourth week my body had become adjusted to the smaller amount of caffeine being consumed and quitting altogether was pretty easy. I only experienced some irritability for a couple of days as a result of the complete withdrawal from caffeine, so it was no biggie.

Do the same with any caffeinated drinks that you consume, just gradually cut back by 1 each week until you aren't consuming it anymore.

Sugar:

I know most of you reading this are seeing **sugar** and thinking "Nooooo.... not sugar!!!". Yes, sugar. Sugar itself does not necessarily cause anxiety (it also sort of can). But it is known to make anxiety symptoms worse because of the effects it can have on your body and mind.

There have been a couple of research studies done in the last 15 years on the effect of sugar on rats that actually showed a correlation between consumption of sugar and anxiety. One study had rats binge on sugar before a period of fasting, after binging on the sugar they all displayed signs of anxiety. The other notable study had one group of rats being fed sucrose while another group was being fed more healthy honey (complete with its anti-oxidant properties). The rats that were fed the sucrose tested as being more prone to suffer anxiety.

Well that's interesting, but we are human beings not rats. So let's just take a quick look at how sugar affects our body and brains in relation to the feelings of anxiety.

By the way... sugar is put into almost everything that we eat and drink. Just look at the ingredient list on any food or drink item that you buy at the store that is packaged in some way. I challenge you to find a loaf of bread in your grocery store that doesn't have sugar in it. I was blown away the first time I saw that sugar was in every single loaf of bread in my grocery store, even the ones that were being baked fresh in the store's bakery... even the ones that were being marketed as organic! Sugar is put into everything from bread to ketchup to frozen pizza and everything in between. Unless you are preparing your own meals mostly from scratch, you are consuming way more sugar than you realize.

When you eat sugar, especially a lot of it, there are some intense things going on in your body and brain. *Small amounts* of natural sugar are not only okay, but are necessary for your body and brain to function properly. Both body and brain use sugars as fuel, so to speak. There is a lot of ongoing research into whether or not this is 100% true, as there are studies showing that our bodies and brains can also use fats as fuel instead of sugars. It's already known that our body and brains do use fats as fuel, but whether or not they can completely replace sugar as our fuel source is still being researched. That being said, I will still advocate that small amounts of natural sugar is still okay and will not cause anxiety or make it worse.

But why is too much sugar, especially things like refined white sugar and high fructose corn sugar, so bad for us and how does it cause or worsen anxiety? There are more reasons than you could imagine, we'll cover a few of them here.

High levels of sugar cause inflammation in your body and brain. Research has shown that sugar is at the root cause for chronic inflammation, which affects the immune system, your brain and other systems of your body. Research further shows that inflammation has been implicated in anxiety and depression.

Additionally, research shows that sugar suppresses activity of a hormone called BDNF. A 2015 study showed that impaired BDNF production creates a vulnerability factor for anxiety disorders. BDNF is found to be low in individuals with depression, meaning that sugar can further lower levels of this hormone. Depression and anxiety often go hand in hand, so consuming lots of sugar can be a really big problem here.

Another reason why too much sugar is bad for anxiety and depression is because of the sugar-rush and crashes that occur. When you eat too much sugar, especially refined sugars or refined carbohydrates, there is an increase of glucose in your system. That initial glucose-rush seems to provide extra energy and alertness, but what is going on inside during that rush and the subsequent crash is pure drama for your system.

Yes, this sugar does give you a boost of energy, but just for a short time. And you usually feel good during this 20 to 30 minute period because the sugar creates a surge of "good mood" chemicals in your brain, releasing dopamine and serotonin. It's actually the same effect that cocaine produces. But soon after eating that cupcake or drinking that super-sized soda the crash effects begin. Your blood sugar levels can then drop quickly, as your insulin levels are increased, which can put your body into stress-mode. As I have already discussed in an earlier chapter, stress causes your body to produce more cortisol, among other things, which can interfere with your body's ability to produce its "good mood" chemicals. Sending you into a downward spiral of feeling bad... such as anxiety and depression. This is why many people just eat more sugar or carbs... to make themselves feel good again for a short period of time, but then they just crash once again. It becomes a vicious cycle where the person becomes physically ill and the anxiety and depression can get worse.

Before the short-lived sugar rush is even done, the effects of the crash can begin with symptoms such as dizziness and blurred vision. These can be followed by other symptoms such as irritability, fatigue, excessive thirst, forgetfulness, poor concentration, insomnia, digestive problems, excessive sweating and depression. Some people may even experience crying spells as a result of the crash. All of the negative symptoms and feelings can add to your anxiety.

I've read from more than one source that consuming a lot of refined sugars and carbohydrates also uses up your mood enhancing B vitamins. Your body uses its B vitamins to turn sugar into energy. So if you are constantly eating foods with refined sugars or carbohydrates you are quickly using up your B vitamins. Research has shown higher levels of depression and anxiety in people that have sugar and carbohydrate rich diets than in people who eat more of a whole foods type of diet. Those B vitamins that are supposed to be helping you produce "good mood" hormones are in short supply, and this adds to your anxiety.

As I mentioned earlier, one of the effects of the sugar crash is insomnia. It's a well researched and documented fact that poor sleep can cause both anxiety and depression. So this just makes everything even worse.

The bottom line here is that sugar not only increases anxiety and depression symptoms, but can very well be one of the causes for a person's anxiety or depression. I'll give you some easy to follow suggestions at the end of the chapter to help you reduce the bad sugars and carbohydrates in your diet to help you be well on your way to being anxiety free.

Artificial Sweeteners:

So I've just told you that eating refined sugars is bad for you for so many reasons including causing and/or worsening anxiety and depression. Maybe you thought to yourself "no biggie… I'll just start eating foods with artificial sweeteners to satisfy my sweet tooth". If you were thinking something along those lines, well, I have some news for you that you are not going to like.

Most artificial sweeteners are really bad news. So many artificial sweeteners are so bad for you I have no idea how they even got approval to be put into our foods and drinks. I won't go into all the reasons why they are bad for you in this book, but I will tell you why they are bad for your anxiety.

Most artificial sweeteners are neurotoxins that disrupt normal nervous system and brain function. Aspartame, the common ingredient that's found in products like diet soda, blocks the production of the neurotransmitter serotonin. As you should know by now, serotonin is one of your "good mood" hormones and you don't want anything to block production of this. This means that it can cause anxiety symptoms and it makes existing anxiety symptoms even worse. In addition, this can cause you to experience headaches and insomnia.

Artificial sweeteners are also Vaso-Constrictors, causing blood vessels to constrict, therefore reducing the supply of blood to certain parts of the body and brain. You may remember that all of the stress hormones also cause your blood vessels to constrict, which adds to your feelings of anxiety.

I would suggest avoiding artificial sweeteners like the plague. I would almost rather have the plague than be forced to consume artificial sweeteners the rest of my life.

Processed Foods, White Flour & Starches:

I'm not going to write too much about this one, mostly because there are already so many books out there that discuss just this one topic. I do feel that I need to at least bring this to your attention in case you are one of the many people in the world who do not know about this.

Processed foods, especially ones made with white flour and/or starches, are not good for you for so many reasons. Yet both are a major part of the average person's diet. Because so many people eat both of these on a regular basis it's hard to imagine not eating them. Yet, cutting these out of your diet, or at least reducing the amounts you eat, will benefit you in so many ways.

I'll cut to the chase… eating anything made with white flour will raise your blood sugar levels. Eating anything with starch added, or eating foods high in starch like white potatoes, will also raise your blood sugar levels. Most processed foods contain processed white flour, starch *and* added sugars… or some combination of them. In fact, if you eat what would be considered an average American diet, you are consuming way too much of all of these. Why is this bad? Scroll back up to the part about sugar for a reminder.

Whether you are consuming sugar, eating foods made with processed white flour or eating very starchy foods… you are increasing the amount of sugar in your body. Refined and highly processed white flour and starches are converted into sugar by your body when you eat them. These sugars are then supposed to be used for energy, but unless you are an athlete who trains intensely every day, your body doesn't need that much sugar for energy.

In fact, when you eat anything with a lot of refined processed flour or starch your sugar levels spike like crazy, and we've already covered why sugar spikes can be bad for you. You will experience the sugar rush and crash that we have already discussed. By the way, the reason why most people get a "food coma" after they eat is because of this… essentially you are experiencing a sugar crash, among other things. Try eating a really big salad for lunch tomorrow and see if you experience a food coma afterwards, odds are that you won't.

I highly suggest that you look for articles or books on the subject of why foods that are highly processed, that are made with processed white flour or are high in starches are bad for you. There are so many more reasons than just the blood sugar spike for avoiding eating these on a regular basis.

Alcohol:

I am very familiar with how alcohol affects anxiety and depression. I am very familiar because I used to self-medicate myself with alcohol. For years it was how I dealt with my anxiety and depression. But the relaxing effects of the alcohol wear off quickly and then make the anxiety and depression even worse. When we do this we end up in a vicious cycle of drinking to feel a little better and then feeling worse, so we then drink to feel a little better and then quickly we feel worse, over and over... wash-rinse-repeat. There is a good chance that you may do this too.

Why do we do this? Because drinking alcohol when we have anxiety or depression makes us feel good, for a little while anyway. The reason why, is because alcohol is a depressant and acts as a sedative, making us feel more relaxed. It causes our bodies to release a greater amount of dopamine, the "happy hormone", thereby disrupting the chemical balance in our brains. This is when we are feeling relaxed and good when we first start to drink alcohol. The anxiety begins to melt away and we feel some relief, and we often even feel happier.

In addition, the alcohol is disrupting things in your brain even further. It interrupts the normal activity of serotonin and endorphins, producing more of them. More "good mood" hormones that initially make you feel relaxed and happy when you start drinking.

Alcohol also increases the production of GABA (gamma amino butyric acid) which is involved in several brain functions, but also is the primary inhibitory neurotransmitter in the brain. This is good to know because a number of medications used to treat anxiety, including benzodiazepines, target GABA. When your brain experiences alcohol, its causing a greater production of GABA, while at the same time it is reducing the brain's stimulatory system (excitability system), making us feel more relaxed and happy.

Our brains try to adapt to these changes by down-regulating the inhibitory system and up-regulating the stimulatory system. When we stop drinking we are left with a brain that's been adapting to alcohol's sedative effects by lowering the inhibitory system and increasing the excitability system.

So what this all means is, as the hours pass by, your brain is working to correct the chemical imbalances that the alcohol has caused. What you then end up with are the feelings of confusion, jitteriness, irritability, anxiety and even depression. Even people who are not anxiety sufferers can experience hangover induced anxiety, which is sometimes referred to as "hangxiety". But if you are already an anxiety sufferer this can just blow your anxiety up, making it feel even worse than it normally does.

Add to all of this the physical aspects of the hangover such as headache, achiness, nausea and tiredness… and you get a very bad day of anxiety that you can't wait to be over. Ah, but we often make the mistake of getting rid of all of that and trying to feel better by drinking again later that day or night. And there you have it, that vicious cycle.

I actually stopped drinking any alcohol for several years, and it helped a lot. These days, now that I have gotten rid of my anxiety, I occasionally enjoy a beer or a glass of wine, and it's not very often. My suggestion to you is if you are experiencing constant anxiety and/or depression, and you drink alcohol on a regular basis, that you quit drinking. You will find that being "dry" helps more than you can imagine. If you feel that you can't completely quit for some reason, at least limit the amount you are drinking so that you don't experience a "hangxiety" attack whenever you do drink.

Nicotine:

I started smoking cigarettes when I was 15 years old. I started smoking because I thought that it was cool, maybe it still was back in 1980 but what did we know back then? I smoked fairly regularly until the age of 38. Fortunately, there were only a few years during that space of time that I smoked more than a pack a day. I actually quit twice during those years, each time for about a year. But most of my smoking was the result of a nervous habit due to my anxiety.

If you are an anxiety sufferer and you smoke cigarettes, you probably get what I mean when I say that smoking "seems" to help. I put the word "seems" in quotes because it is a misconception that smoking helps because it calms you down. It actually has the opposite affect and it's really bad for anxiety and depression sufferers.

Let me clarify that statement a bit. Research has shown that nicotine does have a short term calming effect. The reason why is because nicotine stimulates the release of dopamine in the brain. I'm sure by now you know that dopamine is one of the "good mood" hormones. However, regular nicotine consumption causes the brain to eventually switch off its own mechanism for producing dopamine, so in the long term the natural supply decreases. Low natural levels of dopamine increase anxiety and feelings of depression.

Of course, this is the vicious cycle again similar to drinking alcohol. Smoking cigarettes makes you feel calmer for a very short while, but continued usage causes you to feel worse because you are reducing the amount of dopamine that your system naturally produces, so in order to feel calmer you need to smoke more, over and over, around and around... wash, rinse, repeat. This is one of the real reasons why quitting smoking is so hard. It's not because nicotine itself is extremely addictive, it actually isn't very addictive. It's because of how nicotine effects dopamine production. By the way, cigarettes are loaded with sugar, I'll bet you didn't know that! Smoking sugar has the same effect as eating sugar except that it's a turbo-charged version because smoking it makes it enter your blood stream almost immediately. Believe it or not, if you haven't been able to quit smoking cigarettes its more likely because you are addicted to the sugar in them, not the nicotine.

My "Quit Smoking Forever" program actually discusses the topic of sugar addiction in more detail. By the way, it's part of the reason why many people gain weight when they try to quit smoking!

The Good Things You Should Add

Niacin:

I am sure that most of you have heard of niacin, also known as the B3 vitamin. It is found in almost all multi-vitamins and it is one of five nutrients whose addition is mandatory in all enriched flour and flour products. Niacin is vital to life as a human being, mainly because it helps convert the food that you eat into the energy that you need and it is extremely important for the development and function of your body's cells.

In addition to this, niacin can benefit you in so many other ways including keeping bad cholesterol levels down while raising good cholesterol levels. It improves heart health and can be used to reduce the symptoms of arthritis. It plays a role in over 500 reactions in your body.

But you are probably thinking 'Okay, but what does it have to do with anxiety and depression?'. Good question, and I am about to give you the answer.

During the 1930's in the Southeastern region of the United States there were tens of thousands of Americans who died from a systemic disease called pellagra. The symptoms of pellagra are diarrhea, dermatitis, *dementia*, and death if untreated. The cause of pellagra is essentially malnutrition. Americans living in the Southeast were eating a diet that was high in corn combined with mostly non-nutritious foods, they were severely malnourished.

It was eventually discovered that providing patients with high dosages of multi-vitamins alleviated the symptoms rather quickly, followed by a fast recovery. But in the mid-1930's doctors and researchers found that it was niacin that had the most profound effect. Simultaneously, because the patients being treated for pellagra were suffering from dementia, they also found that niacin was beneficial in treating schizophrenia. Unfortunately, the dosage of niacin needed to reverse the symptoms of pellagra were too low to have an effect on many schizophrenics and the doctors working with pellagra did not think to increase the dosage of niacin to see if that would benefit schizophrenics. You would think that would have been a no-brainer, but I guess back then it wasn't.

But in 1952, Dr. Abram Hoffer and his colleagues conducted clinical trials using niacin to treat patients with schizophrenia. Further studies were conducted shortly afterwards by the same group and the results were nothing short of amazing. Administering moderate to high dosages of niacin to patients with schizophrenia resulted in a 75% recovery rate. That means that 75% of the patients who had schizophrenia *no longer had schizophrenia*! It wasn't until this research had been done that Dr. Hoffer realized that the psychosis experienced by sufferers of pellagra was the same type of psychosis experienced by schizophrenics.

The same Dr. Hoffer used niacin to treat many other patients including some who had been prisoners of war from WW2. These patients suffered from many ailments both physical and psychological. Many of the patients who had been prisoners of war to the Japanese in WW2 had psychological ailments that included severe anxiety. After treating these patients using niacin therapy, the bulk of their ailments improved and most completely went away, including their severe anxiety.

Although you won't read about this in the newspapers or see this on the nightly news, there are doctors who, right now, treat their patients who suffer from psychological disorders with niacin. For many, this is the only treatment that they receive and they recover from their psychological disorders completely.

Some people will notice a difference almost immediately, for others it may take weeks. But, you will know it's working for you because you will feel a noticeable difference in mood. Most of the time you will feel a calmness from the niacin very quickly, even the first time that you take it.

Many parents who know about the benefits of niacin give their child a small dosage B3 vitamin supplement when they notice their child being very irritable or emotionally overwhelmed. The child will just naturally calm down and feel very balanced very quickly.

When taking niacin you may notice your anxiety goes away very quickly or it may take a few weeks, it just depends on what your body needs. But consistent daily use will deliver results whether it's the first time you take it or a little later.

There has been a fair amount of research conducted on how niacin therapy works to essentially cure people of many ailments, including anxiety. The mechanisms involved in the body and brain are too complex for me to explain in this book. But if you would like to learn more about such things I would suggest reading the book "Niacin: The Real Story" by Doctors Hoffer, Saul and Foster.

Let me say now that niacin is a completely safe vitamin for anyone to take. In fact, there are no known deaths from taking niacin, even in very large quantities. That's not to say you should just eat a handful of niacin tablets and see what happens.

First, dosages do matter when you are planning to use niacin to alleviate and help rid yourself of anxiety. Everyone is different, so some people may benefit from a smaller amount than others. That being said, Dr. Hoffer used to prescribe as a therapeutic dosage 3000 mg per day, divided into three 1000 mg amounts taken with meals. Niacin is better absorbed when taken with food. Although you could begin a regimen of niacin using this amount, you may wish to start with much less to see what your body needs and to avoid the "flush" that comes with taking niacin when you first start taking it. It is also suggested to take niacin three times a day because it is water soluble and your body can eliminate it very easily through your urine. It is better to take 1/3 of your daily dosage at a time with meals, rather than one bigger dosage a day.

My suggestion is to start small and work your way up to a larger dosage if you think that you need it. Try starting with just 500 mg a day. If after a week you are not feeling any difference in your anxiety, try 1000 mg a day, and so on until you find the amount that works for you.

Please note that it is believed that you cannot overdose on niacin. There is no known toxic dosage because nobody has ever died from taking niacin. However, a dosage much larger than your body would need can cause nausea. If you did take an amount that your body considered toxic, it would likely induce vomiting to get rid of the niacin anyway. There is no need to try to take niacin in enormous amounts, so no need to try. Likely, you would never have to exceed the therapeutic dosage of 3000 mg per day.

I will make an important note here. Niacin can have an unpleasant side effect on many people called "niacin flush". I have experienced niacin flush when I have taken it, and still sometimes do when I take it these days. Niacin flush is not dangerous, in fact, in many people it can be beneficial.

What is niacin flush? Niacin causes your body's capillaries to dilate, increasing blood flow to your organs and your skin. This is a good thing. However, many people will notice a flush on their skin as it begins to turn red and look much like a sunburn. In addition, this flush can also feel like a sunburn temporarily. Chances are that the first time that you experience the flush, it will feel like a warmth on your skin, but for some it may be more like a 30 minute sunburn. Each time you take niacin the body and skin will flush less, and the temporary sunburn effect will eventually go away. Many people never experience the flush, and others experience it only at first before their body gets used to it. As long as niacin is being taken daily, you will no longer experience the flush when you take it after several days.

The first time that I took niacin I knew about the flush, but nobody told me what it would actually feel like. I remember the top of my head beginning to feel warm, and then the warmth moved down across my face and eventually made its way down to my waist. At the same time my skin felt a little itchy. Within 10 minutes the warm feeling became uncomfortable, like the feeling of a moderate sunburn. I kind of freaked out because I didn't know that it would feel like this. I stood in front of a window AC unit for the next 15 minutes as the sunburn feeling began to disappear. After that I felt fine and noticed that my anxiousness had already gone away. As time went on and I continued to take niacin, I noticed that there were days that I would have no flush at all, and other days that I would have the flush. But the flush was never as bad as that first time.

Before you run out to the store or hop on the internet to buy some niacin, let me quickly explain that there are different types of niacin. The two types that should be taken to treat anxiety are niacin and/or niacinamide. The main difference between the two is that niacin can cause the flush in some people, while niacinamide will rarely ever cause the flush. Niacin has some additional health benefits that niacinamide does not, but other than that they will both be effective at treating anxiety. Both of these types are generally quite inexpensive. I currently take niacinamide daily and I do not experience any flush.

You may also see a "no-flush niacin" for sale that may be another type of niacin that is used by people who cannot tolerate the occasional flush of niacin. It is "inositol hexaniacinate". The downside to this type of niacin is that it usually costs much more than the price of niacin. However, if you just can't stand the feeling of the flush and don't want to wait for your body to eventually get used to it and stop flushing, this could be a good option in addition to niacinamide.

Vitamin D:

Research has shown that vitamin D plays a role in mood regulation and has established a link between vitamin D levels and anxiety disorders and depression.

Certain research studies have shown that people with low levels of calcidiol also experienced symptoms of depression and anxiety. Calcidiol is a byproduct of vitamin D breakdown. If you have low levels of vitamin D you will also have low levels of calcidiol.

Other studies have shown that taking vitamin D supplements can improve both anxiety and depression.

We receive vitamin D naturally from certain foods that we eat as well as from exposure to the sun. I know, weird right? How in the world do we get vitamin D from the sun? Well, we don't actually get the vitamin D from the sun, our bodies produce it when our skin is exposed to the sun. So if you don't get much skin exposure to the sun, which many people these days do not, you will most certainly develop a vitamin D deficiency.

Foods that are high in vitamin D are fatty fish such as salmon, sardines, tuna and mackerel. You can also get a large amount of vitamin D from eating eggs or certain mushrooms such as portabella. However most of us don't eat enough of any of these on a consistent basis to prevent a vitamin D deficiency.

Although I do advocate for people to get more sun exposure and to eat foods like the ones listed above, I highly recommend taking a daily vitamin D supplement. Taking a vitamin D supplement will not only help you in relieving anxiety symptoms, but it will also help you with getting better quality sleep. Good quality sleep is so important to getting rid of anxiety and depression that I have dedicated a section to just that. For now, just know that vitamin D is essential in helping you to get rid of your anxiety.

I personally take 125 mcg of vitamin D every night before I go to bed.

Vitamin B Complex:

So maybe you have never heard that B vitamins can help with your anxiety? Well, most people have not heard this because there haven't been many studies done on the subject until recently.

A 2019 review of 16 trials that included over 2000 participants was conducted to examine the effects of B vitamins on mood. The review of these trials indicated that the majority of them found that the participants who were given B vitamins instead of placebos experienced a "positive effect for overall mood". The majority of the studies that worked specifically with participants who were considered "at risk" (they define "at risk" as being they had a poor diet and or very poor mood) found a significant benefit to mood simply by administering B vitamins.

The review is careful to suggest that vitamin B supplementation is suggested as being beneficial for stress, but not necessarily for anxiety or depression. However, after reading over all of the material in the review, I can't help but believe that the reviewers are just being extra careful to not make a statement regarding anxiety and depression so as to not get into any "hot water" with their peers.

The information in the review clearly points to the fact the vitamin B supplementation did actually work to improve mood in the vast majority of the participants. The reviewers also hint at the fact that vitamin B supplementation could, and perhaps should, also be used for treating those with a "clinical disorder", meaning those with anxiety and depression, among other emotional or psychological disorders.

In addition to this information, many of the B vitamins work well with vitamin D to improve the quality of sleep. Which, as I mentioned before, is extremely important to getting rid of anxiety and depression. There are plenty of other reasons to take a vitamin B complex supplement, but that is not what this book is about. Just know that taking a good vitamin B complex supplement is good for you. I would suggest finding a vitamin B complex supplement that is naturally derived, as opposed to something that is just created chemically in a lab. Quite often the cheap lab created vitamins aren't recognized by your body and you just eliminate them from your body through your urine. You are literally pissing your money down the toilet if you take these kinds of vitamins.

Magnesium:

It is believed that most people are magnesium deficient, as well as just about every other vitamin and mineral the human body needs. But this is important to know because studies have shown that individuals who are experiencing anxiety or depression typically have very low magnesium levels. One study in 1997 conducted on 500 individuals who were self described as feeling depressed were found to be extremely magnesium deficient. Even as far back as 1968, researchers were reporting that magnesium deficiency can cause behavioral disturbances such as depression and anxiety, and that they could be reversed with magnesium replenishment.

Here is where the connection between magnesium and anxiety or depression comes in. Magnesium is necessary for the production of serotonin, one of the "good mood" hormones. With adequate amounts of magnesium the body naturally produces enough serotonin to maintain your emotional balance. Without the proper amount of serotonin in your body you become depressed or experience anxiety.

More on anxiety, if you are already an anxiety sufferer your magnesium deficiency issue is even worse. You see, if you remember earlier in the book I explained that anxiety is mainly caused by prolonged stress, the cause of which can be many. Stress causes magnesium deficiency because adrenaline production uses up magnesium. At the same time, the lack of magnesium causes more stress. The old vicious cycle shows up again.

As a side note, magnesium deficiency can also cause headaches and migraines, leg cramps and other muscle pain, strokes and even heart disease. All things we want to avoid.

Zinc:

Just as with magnesium, researchers have found that many anxiety sufferers have a zinc deficiency. A 2011 study found that the individuals in the study were all extremely zinc deficient. After 8 weeks of zinc supplementation the individuals reported a significant improvement in regards to anxiety symptoms.

Perhaps one of the reasons why zinc is important for anxiety sufferers is that zinc helps with the absorption of magnesium, which you just read about.

Zinc is not to be supplemented in high doses, this is a case of more is *not* better. If you decide to supplement with zinc, most researchers suggest between 25 to 50 mg daily, or even every other day.

Vitamin C:

Does vitamin C really help with anxiety? It can, apparently. The Mayo Clinic states "studies have suggested that oxidative stress may trigger neuropsychological disorders. Antioxidants may play an important therapeutic role in combating the damage caused by oxidative stress in individuals that suffer from anxiety."

Although there hasn't been much study on this subject until very recently, a 2015 study conducted with high school students did provide some unexpected results. A 14 day randomized, double-blind, placebo-controlled trial was conducted on the students where half were given 500 mg of vitamin C per day and the other half received a placebo. The students who received the vitamin C showed reduced anxiety levels as compared to the students who were given the placebo.

More recently, in 2020 a group of researchers reviewed available information regarding vitamin C in stress related diseases and found that vitamin C deficiency is widely associated to stress-related diseases. The researchers noted that several other studies showed that vitamin C supplementation produces an antidepressant effect and improves mood.

Getting large doses of vitamin C every day also boosts your immune system more than you may realize. When you have a healthy immune system you don't get sick very often. When you don't get sick very often you feel better, not only physically but also emotionally.

Amino Acids

You remember dopamine, one of the "good mood" chemicals? When dopamine is released in your body in normal to large amounts, it creates feelings of pleasure and good mood. When it's present in your body and brain at levels below normal, it reduces your motivation and enthusiasm, and... you guessed it, it affects your mood and can create or worsen anxiety.

Tyrosine helps to make dopamine in your body. Tyrosine is an amino acid that is naturally produced in your body from another amino acid, phenylalanine. It's also found in many foods such as chicken, turkey, fish, avocados, almonds, dairy products and many other high-protein foods.

Studies have shown that increasing tyrosine and phenylalanine in your system, either by diet or by supplements, actually increases dopamine levels in your brain. Conversely, if tyrosine and phenylalanine are reduced or eliminated in the diet, and are not supplemented, dopamine levels can become severely depleted. And that spells disaster for your anxiety.

Researchers of a 2011 study conducted in Japan stated that tyrosine regulated anxiety-like behavior in their test subjects. While numerous articles essentially state that tyrosine can help reduce dopamine-related depression, ADHD, and extreme stress.

I have read in various different articles over the past several years about doctors giving some of their patients tyrosine for things such as bi-polar disorder, schizophrenia and ADHD. In one particular case, I read in the book "Dirty Genes" by Dr. Ben Lynch, he prescribed a tyrosine supplement for his own teenager who had ADHD. The results were apparently dramatic. After taking the supplement once a day as prescribed by Dr Lynch, his teenage son no longer exhibited symptoms of ADHD and his son stated that his mood was much better overall.

One important note here, too much L-Tyrosine supplementation can possibly have the opposite effect, affecting mood and symptoms. This would be a case of *more is not better*.

L-Tyrosine supplements can be found online and are relatively inexpensive. I have read several places that 1500 mg per day is the suggested amount and can be taken in the morning or throughout the day. Follow the manufacturer's advice on dosage to make sure and even consider asking a qualified health professional about suggested dosage.

I have taken L-Tyrosine to see if I noticed a difference in mood and it did make me feel better on days that I was feeling stressed out. I do not take it on a regular basis now, as I get plenty of tyrosine and phenylalanine from the foods that I eat now and because I no longer experience anxiety.

A quick note also about another amino acid called tryptophan. I'm sure that many of you have heard of this before and probably know it as the thing in turkey that makes you sleepy. It is found in turkey, as well as many other foods, but it's not usually what makes you sleepy after that giant Thanksgiving dinner (hint: it's all the carbs that makes you sleepy).

Tryptophan is also known to be effective in treating depression, anxiety and even bi-polar disorder. I have read several articles that state that specific amino acids, such as tryptophan, have beneficial   effects on depression, anxiety and insomnia, especially in those diagnosed with bi-polar disorder. It is noted that taking tryptophan 2–3 gm/day may have beneficial effects on anxiety.

In a 2015 study researchers found that changing the diets of the participants to include more L-tryptophan resulted in reduced symptoms of anxiety and depression, as well as positive changes in their mood.

CBD

I'm sure that just about everyone has heard of CBD at this point. CBD (cannabidiol) is a chemical compound and cannabinoid that is found in both hemp and cannabis. CBD is not psychoactive, and most CBD is derived from hemp plants these days. As you may know, hemp is a close cousin to cannabis but it has no THC, the psychoactive compound that is found in cannabis. Even CBD that is derived from cannabis has no THC, so there is no risk of feeling "high" when using CBD. CBD is sold legally in most states at the time of writing this book.

Recent research has found that among the many medicinal and healing properties that CBD has is that it helps reduce the symptoms of anxiety and depression. It doesn't work like some of the other compounds that I have written about, it isn't something that your body needs to function normally. But it has shown promise in recent studies to help alleviate the symptoms of anxiety, so it is worth mentioning here.

For example, a recent study conducted in Brazil was done to test the efficacy of CBD on anxiety. A group of men were asked to do a public speaking exercise, as you may know public speaking is thought to be the number one anxiety inducing activity for most people. Half of the men were given a 300 mg dose of CBD 90 minutes prior to the public speaking exercise and the other half were given a placebo. The half that were given the 300 mg of CBD reported a significant reduction in the anxiety they experienced during the exercise.

Suggestions:

I had mentioned at the end of the section on sugars that I would give some suggestions on how to reduce bad sugars and unneeded carbohydrates, here are a couple.

One of the easiest ways to reduce bad sugars and unneeded carbohydrates is to cook at home instead of going out to eat. I'm not suggesting that you never go out to eat at a restaurant again. But reducing how often you eat out can help you in this area quite a bit.

You see, most restaurants, especially fast food restaurants, serve food that is loaded with sugar, processed flours, starches and tons of unneeded carbohydrates.

The sugar that they put into just about everything makes your food taste a little better. Part of the reason why you think that it tastes better is because you have gotten so used to eating foods loaded with sugar that when you eat something that doesn't have sugar in it, it doesn't taste as good to you. If you start a low sugar eating habit you'll find that when you do go out to eat that you'll notice the sweet taste of everything and it might even seem weird to you.

Order a sandwich from virtually any restaurant and the bread will contain sugar, processed flour and starch... all of which also provide you with many unneeded carbohydrates. Order a side of fries with that and you'll get more sugar and starches, and more carbohydrates. Try a salad instead and the salad dressing on it will be loaded with sugar and more unneeded carbohydrates. Maybe coleslaw or potato salad? More sugar and starches, more carbohydrates. Virtually anything that you will order will contain one or more of these potentially anxiety inducing ingredients in quantities that you don't really want.

So, here is where the suggestion to cook at home more often comes in. You get to choose what goes into your meal and into your body.

If you like to eat sandwiches or burgers try finding bread or buns that don't contain added sugars (or make your own).

Eating salads with dressings that contain little or no added sugars will help tremendously. Or, do what our grandmothers did and make your own dressing. I do it all of the time and most of my dressings taste better than store bought ones.

If you like to eat potatoes, as most people do, switch to potatoes that are waxy since they are less starchy and take longer to digest. Look for yellow potatoes instead of white, they'll always be less starchy.

Another suggestion is to stay away from as much processed food as possible, it's all loaded with added sugars. Check out the ingredients list on everything you typically buy at the store that isn't fresh and processed. You'll be shocked at how virtually everything has sugar in the list, and often it's one of the first items listed which means there is a lot of it. Try slowly switching to more fresh foods, it's actually not that hard if you ease into it.

Making the switch from a mostly processed food diet to a mostly fresh food diet may seem hard at first. It seemed so to me when I did it. But I gradually got used to it and now it would seem very strange for me to eat a lot of processed foods. If you start making the switch, you'll find it often doesn't take that much more time to cook the fresh stuff than it does the frozen or dehydrated processed stuff.

My website dedicated to this program will have more specific suggestions on what you can substitute for the sugar and starch loaded foods that you are most likely eating now, so check it out.

Chapter 5

THE IMPORTANCE OF QUALITY SLEEP

Sleep is an essential part of maintaining a healthy physical body as well as a healthy mind. When both do not get the rest that they need, many complications can arise... including anxiety and depression.

Have you ever had to stay awake for a long time? Maybe you stayed up late to cram for a school exam the next day? Maybe you had to drive a long distance and you didn't get to your destination until early the next morning after driving all night? There could be many reasons why a person has had to stay awake much longer than they usually do and chances are that you have had to as well. Do you remember how you felt after just that one night of being short on sleep?

I know that any time that I have had to stay awake into the wee hours of the next morning and have only gotten a few hours of sleep, I've felt awful the next day. I feel sleepy the entire day, my memory is bad, I can't think straight, I feel physically tired and sometimes even feel like I am sick. I become clumsy… and I feel anxious and sometimes depressed.

Why so many problems from just one night of bad sleep? Studies have shown that virtually every system of the body, especially the brain, is affected by the quality of the sleep a person gets. This is the time that the body and brain essentially repair themselves and without this opportunity they begin to malfunction. So if one bad night of sleep can cause such a problem, what do chronic sleep problems do to your body and brain?

If you are not getting enough quality sleep you have a situation that creates an imbalance in hormone levels, which cause anxiety levels to increase. Lack of sleep can increase your adrenaline levels, which you already know causes feelings of anxiety and even more stress.

A 2019 study conducted to find out the effects of deep sleep on anxiety showed direct links between anxiety levels and deep sleep. Evidence showed that deep sleep restores the parts of the brain that regulates emotions, which helps to prevent escalation of anxiety. It was stated that a new function of deep sleep had been discovered, one that reduces anxiety during sleep by reorganizing connections in the brain, and therefore seems to be a natural anxiety inhibitor.

Of course, if you suffer from anxiety you probably would love to get a good night of deep sleep, but you often can't. I understand this because when I suffered from severe anxiety, not only would I have trouble falling asleep, but I would wake up after 3 or 4 hours of sleep and wouldn't be able to go back to sleep.

I can assure you that if you begin taking supplements that I wrote about in another chapter, you will begin to fall asleep much faster and stay asleep much easier. However, there are a couple of things that I will list here that can also help you to get a good night of sleep. Both are natural and can be taken for short periods of time without any health concerns.

Valerian Root:

Valerian root is exactly what it sounds like it is, the root of the valerian plant. Its calming qualities have been known since the times of ancient Greece, as Hippocrates had written about it way back when. It's known mostly for having both a sedative and anti-anxiety effect. Mostly these days, it is used as a natural herb to promote sleep. Valerenic acid is believed to be the property that stimulates serotonin receptors, which is what produces the calming effect.

Due to its popularity, valerian root can be found in many forms including tea, capsules and tinctures. All of these can be easily found online or even in your local grocery stores, as it is no longer relegated to just vitamin shops. All forms will provide some level of calmness and can help with promoting sleep. However, tinctures tend to be more effective, especially ones that use fresh valerian instead of dried. Although I don't specifically recommend any one brand over another, for the highest effectiveness I would say to look for something like Herb Pharm's Certified Organic Valerian Root Liquid Extract which is also alcohol-free.

You can use valerian root anytime you feel you need a helping hand with falling asleep.

Melatonin:

You've probably heard of melatonin and perhaps you've even used it to help you with sleep. Maybe you have heard of it but never knew what it really was. Melatonin is a hormone, primarily released by the pineal gland, which regulates your sleep–wake cycle. It signals your body and brain when it's time to sleep.

The way this works is that your pineal gland is supposed to release melatonin when it becomes dark outside and then stops when it become light outside. This helps regulate your sleep and is why we naturally sleep at night and are awake during the day.

This melatonin production cycle can get interrupted though. Obviously we have this thing called electricity that allows us to have light inside and outside anytime we want it. Having lots of lights on after it gets dark outside will affect the production of melatonin. But even more so is the effect that blue light has on melatonin production. This blue light is the most troublesome of the light spectrum because it does not get blocked easily by our eyes, and interferes more with the production of melatonin. Blue light is produced by many of our modern electrical devices that we are so used to using these days such as our computer monitors, smartphones and tablets, televisions, and even fluorescent and LED lights.

And we wonder why we can't fall asleep at night!

Of course, it's hard to just shut everything off when it gets dark outside, we live in a modern world where we need to have the lights on and use our devices. But we should take some steps to reduce the amount of light that we receive at night, especially blue light.

Try to not use any of your electronic devices at least an hour before you need to go to bed. Using any of your blue light emitting devices just before you try to go sleep will keep you awake for a while. Get rid of the TV in your bedroom... the last thing that watching TV in bed is going to do is help you to fall asleep.

If you simply can't stay away from your devices for an hour before going to bed consider trying some of these things:

• Getting some blue light blocking glasses. They block the blue light spectrum that is emitted from your devices and they don't affect your vision. They are widely available online.

- Dim the brightness on your devices. If your device has a night mode or dark mode this will help.
- Install and use blue light filtering apps on your devices. This is a good alternative to wearing the blue light blocking glasses.
- Consider not using LED lights. This may be near impossible with incandescent lights being phased out but you can try using a fluorescent light in your bedroom or office because they emit less blue light than LED lights do.

There are also melatonin supplements that can really help when you are having trouble falling asleep or sleeping through the night. I know that when I was experiencing severe anxiety I would occasionally use melatonin a couple of nights in a row to get my body's systems to get back in sync and it really worked wonders for me.

The amount needed is actually less than the dosage in most melatonin pills. Adults don't need more than 5 mg so there is no need to take a melatonin supplement with more than that. Taking more than this can make it harder to wake up in the morning, trust me... I have experienced this. More is not better with melatonin.

Chapter 6

YOUR MIND: THERE'S A LOT GOING ON IN THERE!

What's going on in your mind in regards to your anxiety is *huge*. In fact, many people who suffer from anxiety may only have anxiety because of some of the stuff that's rattling around in their minds. If you tend to be a person who has always been the more sensitive type, then the bulk of your anxiety, in my opinion, is up there in your mind lurking around in your subconscious.

In all of my research the one thing that I always have found is that the bulk of anxiety is being caused by something in the subconscious part of the mind. Many researchers from many different fields have all concluded this. I tend to agree, this is the "big enchilada" when it comes to things that cause anxiety.

Let me quickly give you an example from my own personal research. Way back when I was first starting to look for ways to get rid of my anxiety, I kept reading and hearing about how things that have happened to us in the past continue to affect us in the present. I kept reading that the subconscious part of the mind remembers everything, and therefore it often remembers something that was perceived by us as negative, which continues to affect us throughout our lives. Even if we don't consciously remember these things, they are still being remembered by the subconscious, almost like a program running in the background of our minds.

Traditionally, this type of situation would be approached with psychotherapy, where the person would go to a psychiatrist and they would lie down on a couch and proceed to just talk about things that happened to them in their lives. While the psychotherapist listens and takes notes and makes some comments to help them understand what might have happened in certain situations.

This type of therapy would usually go on for years and years and perhaps never end because the person never gets much out of it other than consciously remembering a lot of different things from the past. In fact, for some people this type of therapy could make things worse. Of course, it could be helpful to some people as they are able to sort and figure out some things about themselves as they talk about the past. But it's hard to consciously fix things that are buried in your subconscious, just remembering a few of them and wishing them away doesn't usually work. Therefore, this is a fairly outdated way of approaching the situation.

I know this may ruffle the feathers of some psychiatrists who still believe in this approach, but it's simply not the most effective approach. What psychotherapy tries to achieve over a long period of time can be achieved in a very short period of time using hypnotherapy, also known as just hypnosis but in a therapeutic manner. Quite a few psychiatrists know this and actually use hypnosis with their patients with a high rate of success.

Hypnosis works so well because it works directly with the subconscious part of our mind. None of us are aware of all the things that our subconscious is aware of. In fact, our conscious mind is designed to work separately from our subconscious mind so it can help us get all of the day to day stuff done, the things that are staring us in the face at the moment.

Here's why… research has shown that we are bombarded with a huge amount of information every second of our lives. To make this easy to grasp, let's refer to everything you could possibly experience as bits of data, like with a computer. There is more data available to us in each second of every experience of our lives than we can possibly perceive or process. Our conscious mind can process up to 50 bits per second. Our subconscious mind can process up to 11 million bits of data per second. That's a hugely ginormous difference!

The subconscious is noticing and processing tons of stuff that we never consciously notice, it is designed to do this. This is a good thing because if we tried to consciously process 11 million bits of data every second we would not only be confused beyond comprehension, we would not be able to function.

The subconscious not only processes tons of information every second but it also remembers everything. Yes, you read that correctly... the subconscious mind remembers everything. Even things that you experienced as a baby are stored in your subconscious. But just because everything is stored there doesn't mean we can easily access it with our conscious mind. There are individuals who have what is called an eidetic memory, more popularly known as a "photographic memory", although that's not a totally accurate description.

There are so few people in the world with an eidetic memory that it's believed that less than 1 percent of the world's population has this ability to remember almost everything they have seen or experienced.

So where am I going with all of this?

As far as your conscious mind is concerned, there are countless things that you have experienced in your life thus far. Whether you know it or not, virtually everything that you have experienced has had a role in forming you into the person that you are today. We are all a combination of genetics and experience. Everything that is *You* is influenced by a combination of your genetics and your life experiences. Based on my research, it's my opinion that our life experiences have more of an influence on "who we are" than genetics.

So let's assume that is true. That means that lots of things that you have experienced throughout your life have caused you to have all of your preferences, perceptions, judgments, and so forth. So if you are an anxiety ridden person, chances are that much of your anxiety is coming from life experiences that you have had. As you already know, anxiety can also be biological and can be helped, or even eliminated, in some people just by changing certain habits and taking specific supplements. It's still my opinion, based on my own experiences and research, that the bulk of anxiety sufferers have their anxiety mostly because of life experiences that were recorded, interpreted and stored in the subconscious part of their mind.

To keep the chapter as easy to read and understand as the rest of the book, I won't go into any details regarding how the subconscious and conscious parts of the mind keep things separate for the most part. Just understand that this is the way that the brain/mind is designed and it works really well most of the time.

For many people though, the problem is that a lot of what they experience is interpreted by their subconscious in a not so helpful way. Much of what we perceive, what we have an opinion about, what we have judgments about, and so on are the result of experiences that occurred during our childhood.

When we begin to develop our perceptions, preferences and judgments as children, these things become absolute truth to us. As children we have no filters... there is nothing in our little minds to tell us that what mommy or daddy is saying is just an old saying they heard from their parents, or that it is something that is just their opinion and that it really isn't a universal truth at all. What we hear, see, taste, smell and feel while we are children become our truth... and these stick with us most, if not all, of our lives. And guess what? You don't even know it because most of it you don't consciously remember... but your subconscious does! And if your subconscious is taking in everything as truth, it sticks there and constantly runs in the background like a computer program.

Our minds, and bodies, operate much like a computer actually. You have an operating system that constantly runs in the background that makes sure that your entire system is running properly... it keeps the heart pumping, the lungs breathing, and so forth. Then you have other programs, like applications that get installed after the operating system. The applications/programs allow you to do many other things than just simply be alive. These help you to do everything from walking and speaking, to determining what your beliefs about the world around you are.

And there you are... programs that get installed during your lifetime, especially the ones in your childhood, are running your life. Of course, many things happen during your lifetime, so additional programs can and do get installed, but they are running on top of the older ones so they just kind of add to what is already going on inside.

Now, maybe as you get older you don't necessarily like the way the programming is running your life. But unless you are a programmer that knows how to change things, those programs just keep running. There is no change, everything stays the same, and no matter what you do consciously you see no results usually.

So what to do... is the outlook bleak? Is there no hope? Of course there is hope, that's why I wrote this book! This is also where hypnosis comes in.

Hypnosis/ Hypnotherapy

You have probably heard the terms hypnotist and hypnotherapist, maybe you've wondered what the difference is? For the most part, people tend to use them interchangeably, and most of that time they are considered the same. I tend to look at these terms a little differently. For me a hypnotherapist is also a hypnotist, but a hypnotist is not always a hypnotherapist.

Here is what I mean. A hypnotist is someone who doesn't work with people primarily to help their clients. Maybe they do some healing work, but they also do street hypnosis or stage hypnosis. They do hypnosis for fun and entertainment.

A hypnotherapist is a hypnotist that works primarily, and usually exclusively, to help people overcome a problem... whether that be smoking, overeating, anxiety, fear of flying, fear of heights or anything else that might be causing a problem in that person's life. For these hypnotists it's all about helping people, and this help is therapy through hypnosis, hypnotherapy. I am in this group.

What It Isn't:

I think that it is important that I explain exactly what hypnosis is *not* because so many people believe that it is something that it is not. I also want to tell any of you that may have had hypnosis before, but got little or no results, that you probably weren't hypnotized properly or perhaps the hypnotist really wasn't qualified.

Most people's experience with hypnosis is limited to seeing a stage hypnotist's show or something that was in a Hollywood movie. They think that being hypnotized means someone having control over them, someone making them do things they wouldn't usually do, or it's some sort of mind control. I can assure you that none of that is true.

Hollywood would have you believe all of that junk because it makes for more interesting movies. If they made a movie based on what hypnosis really is it would be pretty boring for the people watching the movie, and the producers would lose a lot of money. It's just fictional storytelling to make things more interesting and exciting.

Stage hypnotists are another story. I think just about everyone has seen at least one stage hypnosis show, whether in person or on a video. I'll admit they can be pretty entertaining. But what I don't like about stage hypnosis is that it makes everyone think that the hypnotist can somehow make people do anything and everything. The stage hypnotists want everybody to think that this is true, that they control you and make you do anything that they want. But guess what… that's a lie, it's simply not true.

Hypnosis cannot make you a mindless zombie. The first thing that I will tell you about hypnosis is that no hypnotist can ever make anybody do anything that they don't want to do…. *Ever*. Many experiments have been done to see if hypnosis can make people do something that they would never want to do on their own, but results have shown it's virtually impossible.

Hypnosis is not mind control. But you might ask, then why do the hypnotized people on stage do all of the things that the hypnotist tells them to do? They are clucking like chickens, playing air guitar, and barking like dogs. That's a great question, I'm glad that you asked. The answer may surprise you. It's because the people who are hypnotized *want* to do those things.

Have you ever noticed with stage hypnotists how they bring a lot of people on stage at first, and then they slowly begin to tell certain people to go back to their seats? If it's a big audience there might be more than 50 people on stage to start with. Then the hypnotist sends 10 of them back to their seats. Then the hypnotist does a few other little things with everybody and sends another 10 back to their seats. This keeps going on until there are maybe only 10 people left. What's going on here?

The hypnotist is constantly testing everyone to find out several things. The first thing the hypnotist is testing for is how much do you like to have fun in front of a large group of people? If you didn't go up on stage in the first place then you aren't someone who wants to have fun in front of a large audience. So everyone who comes up onto the stage passes the first test.

The hypnotist keeps testing for how much fun you like to have in front of a large group of people because he/she only wants the people who really want to have some fun. The hypnotist is also testing everyone to see how much they *want* to be hypnotized. Obviously, the last thing that the hypnotist wants is to have people on stage that don't really want to be hypnotized.

While all of that is going on the hypnotist is also testing everyone to see how *easily* they can be hypnotized. Again, the last thing that the hypnotist wants is to have some people on stage who are difficult to hypnotize.

So what has happened is the hypnotist started out with a large group of people who passed the first test while sitting in the audience, and then they slowly figured out who the best people to hypnotize were. The stage hypnotist is pretty sure those 10 people left sitting on stage are willing to have a lot of fun in front of a large group of people, they all want to be hypnotized, and they all show signs of being individuals who are easily hypnotized. This is the group who is going to be willing to cluck like a chicken, play air guitar and bark like dogs... or whatever they have them do on stage these days. These 10 people actually want to have this fun, silly and potentially embarrassing stage hypnosis experience! That's why they do all of the funny and entertaining things that the hypnotist tells them to do, *they want to do them.*

I'll give you a quick example of a stage hypnosis act that went wrong to show you why people can't be hypnotized to do something they don't really want to do. I won't give the name of the hypnotist here because it doesn't really matter. This particular stage hypnotist went through everything that I have already described to determine who the ten participants would be. About halfway through the stage show everything seemed to be going well and everyone was doing the funny things that they were being told to do. It was at this point that the hypnotist decided to do one of his gags, where he gets a giant cardboard cutout of a magnifying glass and he places it in the lap of one of the participants, who in this case happens to be a woman. The hypnotist tells the woman that it's a magic magnifying glass and when he snaps his fingers she will look at everyone through this giant magnifying glass and she will see everyone naked, except for the hypnotist. So he snaps his fingers and she picks up the cardboard prop and throws it on the ground. Of course everyone in the audience is laughing because they know that's not what is supposed to happen. So the hypnotist picks it up and puts it back in her lap and tries again. Again, she throws it onto the ground. The audience is laughing because they can see things are not going the way the hypnotist planned and he is nervously joking about the problem. He tries a third time and gets the same result, she throws it to the ground, at which point he realizes this isn't going to work and moves on to the next gag.

After the show, the hypnotist decided to tell the woman what happened. When she found out what he was suggesting to her on stage, she looked at him and said something to the effect of "I would never want to do something like that!". The hypnotist admitted that when this happened on stage he knew that was the case, because the only reason that she wouldn't have done something like that is if it went against something that she believed in, that she probably had a moral problem with seeing a bunch of strangers naked. Proof that you can't hypnotize someone to do something that they don't want to do, even if it's just for fun.

Maybe someone you know has seen a hypnotist to quit smoking but they were never able to actually quit? Chances are that either the hypnotist wasn't properly trained and didn't really know what they were doing, or even more likely it was that the person *didn't really want* to quit smoking. I have heard countless stories of people who went to see a hypnotist to quit smoking because their spouse wanted them to quit smoking. In almost every case the hypnotist told them that hypnosis wouldn't work for them until *they wanted to quit*, it doesn't work because someone else wants them to quit.

In a nutshell, nobody can ever hypnotize you and make you believe something that you don't want to believe, or do something that you don't want to do. Nobody can control you with hypnosis. It just won't work.

What It Is:

Now the fun part... finding out what hypnosis really is! Hypnosis is pretty much a relaxed physical and mental state that allows your subconscious mind to be more easily accessed. It's a lot like when you are sleeping, except that you usually don't fall asleep during hypnosis.

When you are sleeping, your conscious mind is asleep. Yet your subconscious mind is wide awake doing all of the things it needs to do, including dreaming.

I like to think of hypnosis as a dreaming state without being fully asleep. This state of being very relaxed, and in a dream state while not actually being asleep, is called a hypnotic trance. There are different levels of trance and, believe it or not, most people go in and out of hypnotic trances throughout the day without a hypnotist even being involved. That's right, you are practicing self-hypnosis almost every day.

Any time you daydream, you are in a hypnotic trance. Anytime that you are driving down the road and end up at your destination but don't remember the last several minutes of driving because your mind was somewhere else, you are in a hypnotic trance. Even when you watch a movie that you are completely absorbed in and almost forget that you are just sitting on your couch, you are in a hypnotic trance.

These are all forms of self-hypnosis. By the way, all hypnosis is self-hypnosis, actually. You are engaging your subconscious mind through thought and imagination and the conscious mind takes a little break. It's still there listening in, but it's not in control of the predominant thoughts and emotions you are experiencing. It can choose to come back in control anytime if it needs to.

Hypnosis with a hypnotist is pretty much the same thing, except that instead of your subconscious mind thinking about whatever it feels like thinking about, the hypnotist guides your subconscious to think about specific ideas and scenarios.

With the exception of when you are in an exceptionally deep trance, your conscious mind is still aware of what is going on, it's still listening in. You are still always in complete control and you can wake yourself up if you really want to.

I had mentioned already that there are different levels of trance. Let me explain this in a general way so that you know what I mean by this, there is no need to go into a deep definition of each in this book. In my opinion and experience, there are basically 4 levels of trance.

- Light Trance- This would be similar to when you are daydreaming. Your conscious mind is just taking a little break while you engage your subconscious mind in imagination. You are lightly relaxed. You can easily pop out of this type of trance for any reason, even a little noise outside the room can cause you to come out of trance. This isn't a particularly useful trance state for hypnotherapy.
- Medium Trance- Similar to the light trance but more relaxed in both your body and mind. Just like with the light trance, your

conscious mind is still taking a little break, but it's a little more out of the way. It's still listening to everything that is being said by the hypnotherapist but you are less likely to just pop out of trance for any little reason. Many hypnotists work with this trance state.

• Deep Trance- Similar to the medium trance but even more relaxed in both your body and mind. Your conscious mind is still aware of things but it's much less likely to interfere with the hypnotherapy. The conscious mind can still wake you out of trance if it wanted to, but generally it's not going to unless it just really doesn't like something that's going on. This is the trance state that many hypnotherapists work with because this is when the subconscious mind can really respond well to the therapy.

• Exceptionally Deep Trance- Similar to the deep trance but with complete body and mind relaxation. The conscious mind is usually not aware of things and it is essentially sleeping. The person is not truly asleep, because their subconscious mind is fully engaged with the hypnotherapist. This trance state is not used by most hypnotherapists because it's usually not necessary, but it can be beneficial for some people depending on what they want to achieve.

When I work with clients I generally have them in a deep trance state. This is also known as the somnambulistic state. This is where the subconscious mind is very open to communication and receptive to positive suggestion. Everybody can go into a deep trance state, but some will go into this state much easier than others. In fact, about 10% of the population are what is referred to as being a "natural somnambulist". A natural somnambulist is someone who very easily goes into this deep level of trance.

Natural somnambulists do extremely well with hypnotherapy because they enter into deep trance quickly and their subconscious is more easily receptive to the hypnosis process. Stage hypnotists try to find natural somnambulists in the group that they have on stage because they will be the easiest to work with. That's why they do all of that "testing" on stage with everyone before they pick their final participants. Usually, some of the people left on stage are natural somnambulists.

But, that is not to say that if you are not a natural somnambulist that you won't be able to go into a deep trance state. You can, it just means that you are like most people; it takes a little longer to get you into that very relaxed and receptive state.

There are some people who have trouble being hypnotized, or who think that they can't be hypnotized. What this usually means is that the person just has a hard time relaxing enough to go into a deep hypnotic trance. Often times, someone who might label themselves as a "control freak" has trouble being hypnotized because they just can't relax enough about everything to easily go into hypnotic trance. It's been estimated that 15% of the population have difficulty being hypnotized below a light trance.

But for any of you that think you fall into this last group, have no fear! Everyone can be hypnotized because, remember, everyone goes in and out of a hypnotic state on their own every day. You are practicing self-hypnosis every day without even knowing it. And all hypnosis is self-hypnosis. The hypnotherapist is just guiding you. It may take a little more effort or even a couple of tries, but if you want to be hypnotized you can be, it's not hard.

How Hypnosis Gets Rid of Anxiety

So, I've gone over what hypnosis is, what it isn't and how your subconscious mind remembers everything that you have ever experienced and replays it all like a program in the back of your mind. Now I'll explain how and why hypnosis works so well to get rid of anxiety and many other problems in people. I'll explain this in a very general manner so it's easy to understand, even though it's really not all that complicated in the first place.

So, as I explained in the beginning of this chapter your subconscious mind is always "turned on" and working, it's able to process 11 million bits of data every second and it remembers everything.

The subconscious mind believes everything that it is told when you are a child, usually up until the age of 7. So anything that you have seen or experienced is remembered based on your understanding of things at that time. Your parents, neighbors, teachers and so on are constantly telling you things based on their own opinions and interpretations of their world. So whatever they are telling you is being remembered as truth by your subconscious when you are a child.

So if you were unfortunate enough to have parents that told you many negative things when you were a child, such as that you are stupid, or lazy, or won't ever be successful in life... your subconscious learned that to be truth and that became your belief. It becomes a program that runs in the background of your mind. This happens with anything that you experienced during those impressionable years. That's the term that people often use for when you are a child, the impressionable years, because it's during that time that you are learning everything, and believing everything, that you are experiencing.

So all of that stuff that your subconscious recorded as truth is there in your mind playing like a program, and it generally doesn't ever go away. But it doesn't just stop at age 7, oh no. After the age of 7 you start using your conscious mind to help you determine what you believe and what you don't believe. But, you are still very impressionable about many things as you grow older. You just keep adding to the programs that are in your mind and are being believed by your subconscious.

This goes on for most of your life. If your experiences early on in life were mostly negative, then your subconscious belief system will tend to continue to believe mostly negative things. If you have spent most of your life focused mostly on negative beliefs you are more than likely going to develop some emotional issues. Anxiety, depression, low self-esteem and low self-worth are among the issues that are likely to develop. If these issues are deeply rooted in the subconscious, they are not ever going to go away on their own.

You can consciously try get rid of such beliefs, but that doesn't tend to work and any positive results are generally very short lived. Things like positive thinking, positive affirmations, reading lots of positive suggestion books are all examples of ways that people try to consciously change their subconscious beliefs and programming. These are all good things, but if you're experiencing severe anxiety or depression they don't get deep enough to fix things. It's like trying to put a band-aid on a bullet wound to stop the bleeding.

Your conscious mind has very little control over your subconscious mind, especially when you are an adult. The conscious part of the mind more or less has been trained to go along with what the subconscious has been trained to believe. But even if you consciously disagree with what you believe and feel deep down inside, it's not enough to change things much. Your subconscious mind runs the show, not your conscious mind.

This is where hypnotherapy comes in and becomes such an amazing way to resolve many of these issues, especially anxiety.

Hypnotherapy allows a properly trained hypnotherapist to contact your subconscious directly without the conscious mind trying to interfere. Simply by having a person relax their body and mind and become calm, the conscious mind can be made to take a little break. With the conscious mind taking its "coffee break", the hypnotherapist can have a person relax even more until they reach that deep trance state where the subconscious is actively listening without interference from the conscious part of the mind.

Here is the important part, as long as *you want the change,* in your beliefs and perceptions or whatever the problem may be, your subconscious will be open to changing the old ones. As long as you want the change your subconscious will allow it.

There are a number of different types of hypnosis, some of them work better than others for anxiety and depression. It's my opinion that the best type of hypnosis for anxiety and depression is a combination of direct and indirect hypnosis. This is what I use in my prerecorded hypnotherapy sessions that are part of my anti-anxiety program. There are some instances when a person would benefit more from a live hypnotherapy session than prerecorded sessions, but when done right the prerecorded sessions work well for the vast majority of people.

So, how long does this take? Well, a lot has to do with the person who has the anxiety. A natural somnambulist will almost definitely only need to listen to each of my prerecorded sessions one time. Many people who are not natural somnambulists will also only need to listen to each of my prerecorded sessions one time. Then there are others who may need to listen to each of the recordings more than one time. If you are one of those people, don't be concerned, there is nothing wrong with you. It simply means that you may not have gone deep enough into trance, or your subconscious needs a bit more suggestion to make the change in old beliefs and programming. But rest assured, as long as you really want the change it will happen.

Sometimes people would rather have a live hypnotherapy session, and sometimes that makes sense for people who have had a lot of traumatic things happen to them. This usually involves the same direct and indirect suggestion hypnosis but will almost always include age regression and/or parts therapy.

Age regression is simply having the subconscious mind go back in time to memories of things that caused the negative beliefs and programming and to see them from a different perspective, so that the subconscious mind can interpret them in a different way. Changing the way the subconscious interprets the things that were experienced in the past is a powerful way to get rid of anxiety.

Parts therapy is having the subconscious reveal certain aspects of the person's personality, or parts of the subconscious, that may be causing the anxiety. This is not saying that a person has multiple personalities! We all have different parts of our subconscious that act as personalities within the subconscious. These parts exist to help us with many things. Sometimes there are parts that are trying to help us, but they are actually going against what we now want and what is truly good for us. Parts therapy actually has the subconscious discover which parts are doing things that aren't really helping, and has them change so that they do actually help. It sounds kind of strange but it's actually quite interesting. Many people remember what happened during the hypnotherapy session and think it's pretty cool.

I'll still do live hypnotherapy sessions with people, so I leave that option open to everyone as well. But having a number of prerecorded sessions to listen to in the comfort of your own home is probably the best option for most people. I also do custom hypnotherapy session recordings for those clients who want the personalized detail that comes with a live session, but without having to travel to my office for an in-person visit.

I can't stress enough how effective hypnosis is at getting rid of anxiety in people. It can do so much more than just get rid of anxiety as well. Hypnosis is probably the best way to deal with many causes of depression, fears and phobias of any kind. Hypnosis can be super effective with other issues such as quitting smoking, losing weight and healthy eating, improving self confidence and self esteem, being more success minded, and so on. The list is pretty much endless. Hypnosis is pretty miraculous!

Hypnosis is really an amazing art and science that is still underappreciated. I do believe that the 21st century will usher in a new era of using hypnotherapy to help people with the many problems that exist and that it will become much more commonplace.

Chapter 7

EXERCISE AND NATURE

Love it or hate it, Exercise is necessary!

I don't know why, but anytime I have read a book or watched a program where they say that I need to exercise, I cringe. I don't necessarily hate exercise, but I don't like people telling me that I have to do it.

I guess it's because when I hear that, I have an image of having to go to a gym and having to work out on weight machines, and do lots of push-ups and sit-ups. The gym is just not my thing... so I have an internal protest to the suggestion that I need to exercise.

But exercise doesn't have to be the gym. It can be virtually any type physical activity. I particularly like to go on walks in local parks and going on day hikes in the nearby mountains. When I get the opportunity I also like to go on multi-day hikes, swimming and sometimes skiing. I am more interested in being outdoors and moving around, I am not a big fan of being indoors and being in one place doing repetitive exercises. But I know many people do like the gym, and that's cool for them, just not for me.

Okay, so why does exercise help with anxiety and depression? Well, you remember those "good mood" hormones and chemicals that I keep writing about? Research has shown that exercise causes your body to release endorphins that enhance your natural sense of well being. According to the Mayo Clinic, "natural cannabis-like brain chemicals (endogenous cannabinoids)" are released during exercise and are part of the reason why you feel good after exercising.

Exercise also works to relieve anxiety and depression by improving sleep in most individuals. As you read in an earlier chapter getting a night of good quality and deep sleep on a regular basis is necessary when trying to relieve your anxiety.

Believe it or not, research has shown that even a brisk 15 minute walk each day can begin to provide you with everything mentioned above. Of course, for best results you'll want to do that brisk 15 minute walk every day. You can find 15 minutes a day to go for that brisk walk, can't you?

The Power of Nature

Simply being surrounded by nature can lower your stress levels and alleviate symptoms of anxiety and depression. Maybe you have read something about this at some point in your life. There is actually a field of research that is called ecotherapy that studies this subject.

Ecotherapy research has shown a strong connection between time spent in nature and reduced stress, anxiety, and depression. Although researchers in this field have yet to determine a clear reason why time spent in nature can have such a profound effect, a 2015 study was able to show that spending time in nature, as opposed to spending time in urban areas, lowered activity in the prefrontal cortex region of the brain. This region of the brain is active during times of having repetitive thoughts that focus on negative emotions.

Just exactly what causes the prefrontal cortex region to calm down is still unknown. However, it is believed to have to do with the calming sounds of nature, or even the silence in nature, that naturally lowers blood pressure and cortisol levels. (You remember that stress hormone cortisol?) It's also believed that the visual aspects of nature have a calming effect on us all. Nature is not only pleasant to look at, but it distracts us from the negative thoughts that we might normally be thinking.

Another reason why it's so important to take time out to spend in nature is that we are genetically programmed to want to be in nature. It's our natural setting and something inside us all just needs to be near it and among it to feel balanced. Just how that works, I don't know, I'm not a geneticist.

But think about this… when we are in the sunshine our body produces its own vitamin D, which is necessary for us to stay alive. When we are outside and we breathe a lot of fresh air we feel relaxed and can even get sleepy from it. Our bodies want to be outside and in nature as much as possible because that's where we function the best.

I'd like to add couple of other things here because I think that its good information for everyone to know.

There is an aspect of being in nature that most people are not aware of. It has to do with the Earth's resonant frequency. A resonant frequency is basically when something gives off an energetic frequency that causes a specific rate of vibration. Almost everything in the universe gives off and responds to resonant frequencies. Just think of this as being similar to sound and its vibrations.

The Earth produces a resonant frequency called the Schumann Resonance. This was discovered by Otto Schumann through mathematical calculations in 1952. Since then research has been done to try to either prove or disprove this discovery. In recent years many researchers have concluded that this Schumann Resonance does exist and it is the cause for many things that happen on our planet.

The Schumann Resonance is considered the "heartbeat" of the planet. Interestingly enough, human being's natural resonant frequency matches that of the Earth.

Many scientists consider the effects of this particular frequency on life itself. Luc Montagnier, a Nobel Prize award-winning scientist, found that DNA strands responded to and communicated with each other when he applied the resonant frequency of the Earth. It was only at this resonant frequency that this happened! This one experiment is just part of the ever growing amount of scientific proof that we are energetically connected to and affected by the Earth, and nature.

There have been other research experiments done to determine the effects that the Schumann Resonance has on humans. Several such experiments in Germany were conducted between 1964 and 1989 on over 400 individuals. The individuals were asked to live for a time in a so-called isolation apartment. The apartment was shielded from external variations in light, temperature and electromagnetic fields. After some time inside this isolation apartment, anywhere from days to weeks, many interesting things occurred to the participants including disruptions in endocrine function, thyroid function, depression and other affective disorders.

However, when a machine that resonates at the Schumann Resonance of 7.83Hz was placed in the apartment, the individuals found that their discomfort, depression and illnesses disappeared or were mostly alleviated. Proving that our human bodies need to experience nature... natural light, air and the Earth's resonant frequency.

Being outside in nature allows us to be more directly exposed to the Earth's resonant frequency.

Another healthy aspect of being in nature that may surprise you is something that many people are referring to as "Earthing" or "grounding". It's likely that you have at least heard of it since in recent years there have been many more people researching it and writing about it.

Similar to the Schumann Resonance, the Earth itself creates energy and provides a vast supply of electrons on the surface of the Earth. Recent research has found that connection with the Earth's electrons promotes positive physiological changes and well-being. Earthing is the practice of connecting with the Earth's constant supply of electrons on its surface.

A 2012 study that reviewed multiple research studies on the potential benefits of "Earthing", showed Earthing to be a simple and profoundly effective way to relieve or dismiss issues with disorders such as chronic stress, anxiety, inflammation, pain, cardiovascular disease and sleep disorders, among a host of other issues. I'm not sure that Earthing alone will cure a person of any specific issue or disorder, but there is proof out there that it can definitely help.

Unfortunately, even when most of us go outside in nature and experience all of its benefits, we don't usually get the full benefit of the Earth's vast supply of electrons or energy. Modern day life has unintentionally interfered. Guess what... the floor in your apartment, house or office interferes with the Earth's energy and it can't really get to you. Even your shoes interfere with its ability to reach you. This is because the bulk of this energy comes from within the Earth and sits at the surface on the ground.

One way that you can receive the full benefits of the Earth's energy is to take some time each day to stand barefoot on the ground. Now, I don't mean in your apartment or house, I mean outside on the ground. Find a patch of grass, sand, dirt or even plain concrete and stand on it barefoot for a while. At least 30 minutes is best, but even if you can't squeeze 30 minutes in each day any amount will help. If you can't bear to just stand outside, you can sit or lie down as well, but make sure that some part of you that has exposed skin is touching the ground. Wood, carpet, asphalt, sealed or painted concrete and vinyl won't work and will block the flow of the Earth's energy that you are trying to connect with. So standing on them won't work.

There are products for sale on the internet that supposedly allow you to get the Earth's energy through a mat you can stand or sleep on while inside your house. I have never tried using any of these products so I am not sure how effective they are, but they might be worth a try if you don't have much time to stand in the grass or if it's too cold where you live most of the year.

Chapter 8

OUTSIDE INFLUENCES

As I had listed earlier in the book there are many different things that can cause or add to the causes of your anxiety. Some of these things are harder than others to avoid. But there are things that you can avoid, or at the least reduce your exposure to, in an effort to help get rid of your anxiety.

The News

As I am sure you have noticed, "the news" is filled with mainly negative stories. With the communication technology that the 21st century has given us, the ability to know what is happening everywhere in the world at any given moment makes learning of negative news almost constant. Now we get to know about horrible things happening not only in our own country, we get to know about everyone's tragedies and struggles as well... how fun! As a result, many of us are more stressed out than ever before.

It used to be that you only got your daily dose of negative news when you had some time to read the newspaper, or maybe while listening to a little bit of news on the radio while driving to and from work, or watching your TV at 11:00 when the nightly news came on. That gave everyone plenty of opportunities to hear about all the negative things going on in their community and the big stuff that may have happened world-wide.

Ah, but now we can have a constant stream of negativity because we can access it all on our phones or tablets that we always have with us. Not only that, but the laptops we use at work or at home give us additional access. It's all connected via the internet and we have 24 hour access to all of the worst and most negative stuff going on in the world being presented by hundreds of thousands of online platforms and outlets. And people wonder why they are stressed out!

I had a coworker not that many years back who was completely addicted to what was going on in the world. He had his smartphone, his tablet and a laptop in the office with him. He was constantly checking each one all day long. I asked him one day why he always brought all three with him to work and he answered something along the lines of "I'm afraid that if I don't have access to all of the websites that I am interested in that I will miss something, so I have each device logged in on the websites I think are most important". I don't remember all of the websites that he mentioned needing to monitor but one of them was Facebook. Lots of negative news and personal drama is available on Facebook. Needless to say this coworker seemed a bit stressed out most of the time.

I had been a news junkie in the past as well and I noticed that after an hour or two of reading mostly negative news I felt an increase in stress and anxiety. If I decided to waste even more of my day with reading the news or watching news videos, I would almost feel depressed at the end of the day. I finally realized that I didn't need to know everything that was going on in the world. My knowing about it wouldn't change any of it. My knowing about it just made me feel bad and increased my stress and anxiety.

Now, I am not going to suggest that you completely cut yourself off from all news, but... you do not want to inundate yourself with it. It's smart to want to stay informed, but... you don't need to be informed about everything happening in the world. Essentially, you need to cut yourself off from as much negative news as possible. This may feel difficult at first, but it will get easier with time.

What I started doing to wean myself off of too much negative news was this... I would limit myself to a certain amount of time each day that I could read the news or watch news videos. Usually I would give myself less than an hour. I also gave myself the option of taking an entire day off from any news at all.

On the days that I gave myself time to look at the news, I would purposely avoid reading the stories that had the worst sounding headlines. Sometimes I would just ask myself "Do you really need to know about that?".

I got myself to the point where I was only reading about things that were very important to me or were not negative in the first place. I started using some of the extra time that I now had to read about positive things that I was interested in (like how to get rid of anxiety!). Very quickly I found that by doing this my stress levels were much lower, which resulted in less anxiety.

You see, by constantly inundating ourselves with negative things, we create for ourselves a negative world. When we live in a world of constant negativity we increase our stress, the stress hormones kick-in and, well, it's no wonder we develop anxiety and can't get rid of it.

Surrounding yourself in negative news creates a negative world for you. Which then creates more subconscious programs that run in the back of your mind that are constantly telling you how negative everything is. When you are constantly looking at your world through a negative lens, life is much harder than it needs to be. It also creates more stress, anxiety and eventually depression.

Believe it or not, you are in control of how you see your world.

Movies and TV

That last line that you just read… is so very true. So, going along with avoiding as much negative news as possible, I also have to suggest that you avoid negative movies and TV as much as possible. You may think that this suggestion is a bit crazy, but it's not.

Many years ago I used to watch a lot of true crime TV shows and I watched a lot of movies that were action and drama with lots of violence and sometimes even quite depressing plots. I, like many people, found it all to be entertaining. But I also noticed something else… I always felt bad after watching this stuff.

I'm not sure that I can find an accurate word for exactly how I felt after watching a lot of that stuff… but it was a very negative feeling. Sometimes I could be affected for days after seeing certain movies.

At some point while working on getting rid of my anxiety and mild depression I figured out that watching all of this negative stuff wasn't helping me. So I performed an experiment.

I decided to stop watching anything that had a lot of negative themes: horror, violence, murder, rape, crime, war, or anything destructive like doomsday themes. I started only watching comedies or things with light hearted themes. I also started watching more documentaries on things like travel and science. Basically I was doing whatever I could to avoid watching anything that was negative.

And you know what? I noticed a big difference. No more negative feelings after watching something and no more being affected by some of it for days. I realized that although this alone would not get rid of my anxiety, it certainly was helping.

I realized that when we watch a movie or show, we go into self-hypnosis (as I have already mentioned in the section on hypnosis) and our subconscious is being given ideas, concepts and emotions to think about and remember. Watch something negative and you are feeding your subconscious negative things to absorb and think about and perhaps even create a new program to run in the background of your mind. Consistently watch negative things every day and you are guaranteed to influence the way your subconscious mind defines your world.

The bulk of the movies and TV shows that come out each year have quite negative themes. Much of the world's population watches these negative movies and shows. I used to hear co-workers talking about all the things that they watched over the weekend and the bulk of it was negative themed. And those people wonder why they have emotional issues!

My suggestion is to simply cut back on all of the negative things that you watch at first. Like anything else, it's often hard to just go "cold turkey" and stop completely on day 1 of trying. If you think you want to try that, go for it. But if not, just cut back to start with. After a couple of weeks cut back even more. See if you notice a difference in the way that you feel after not watching anything negative for a few days.

To this day, I am at the point where I rarely watch anything with a negative theme. I do occasionally watch something that looks like a good sci-fi drama or action flick, but I try hard not to watch anything super-negative.

Video Games

I'm not going to say much here other than the fact that negative themed video games can have the same effect on you as negative themed movies and shows. In some ways they are worse because you are actively involved when playing a video game as opposed to just watching a movie or show. This active involvement makes everything that you are experiencing more real to your subconscious and therefore has a better chance of affecting you.

If you are really into gaming I can understand how avoiding negative or violent games might be difficult. If nothing else, cut back on them, it will help you more than you can imagine.

Chapter 9

RELEASING TRAPPED EMOTIONS

When I was initially looking very seriously into how to get rid of my anxiety back in 2008, I accidentally came across something very powerful. I was reading a book about the law of attraction, which was a rather new concept to me at the time. The book that I was reading was about how to be more specific in making the law of attraction work for you.

At the beginning of the book, the author stated that you have to be in a positive frame of mind before you ever get the law of attraction to work for you in positive ways. Basically he was stating that if you are anxiety ridden or depressed, you'll never be able to attract many positive things through the law of attraction. The author suggested that before even reading any more of his book, to get help with any anxiety or depression first. His suggestion was not to go see a psychiatrist, however.

Instead, the author suggested a couple of things including learning how to release trapped emotions. He suggested a couple of very specific programs, and I decided to try one of them. It is called the Sedona Method, initially developed by Lester Levenson. In a nutshell, it's a rather simple method to detach and release unwanted emotions from memories, beliefs or ideas in your mind. They don't have to be negative emotions, they can be any emotion that you want to release, but that's what I was going for.

I found the whole concept very interesting and decided to try it. The basic process was a bit difficult for me at first, even though the process itself is very simple. However, after a few days of practicing I found the process to be pretty easy.

Using this method, I slowly peeled away some of the layers of anxiety that were associated with negative beliefs that I had. It was a combination of releasing emotions using the Sedona Method and using certain types of hypnotherapy that really turbo-charged my efforts to rid myself of anxiety.

Even if the concept of releasing emotions attached to some of your beliefs seems a bit odd, I highly recommend trying it.

I do want to bring one other method of releasing trapped emotions to your attention. I came across this only a few years ago and it helped me tremendously with some of the anxiety that continued to nag me and not go away. This method is called the Emotion Code, developed by Dr. Bradley Nelson.

The Emotion Code is based on something called "muscle testing" to find out what emotion is trapped inside you in regards to specific issues that you have. The idea is that some emotions can get trapped in your body as energy, which can cause all sorts of problems for you. The resultant problems can be psychological or physical. By finding out specifically what emotion is causing the problem, and where the energy from that emotion is stuck inside of you, you can easily release it and potentially be free of your problem. It sounds a little strange, but believe me, it works. I can attest to that.

Conclusion

CONCLUSION

So, you have read about a lot of ways to help you get rid of your anxiety. Maybe your head is spinning with all of this information. Maybe you are wondering how on Earth you can possibly do all of these things. Don't despair, you don't have to put everything into play today.

My suggestion to you is to start with some of the things that seems the easiest to you. Maybe for you taking supplements and avoiding the news will be easiest to start with. Perhaps getting outside for some exercise, cutting out caffeine and getting deep restful sleep at night will be the easiest. Just pick a few things to start with and notice any improvements.

Whatever you choose to start with, whether it be a couple of things or many things, I do suggest that you include hypnotherapy. Hypnotherapy for anxiety is going to be one of the most effective ways to get rid of your anxiety, hands down. It's my opinion and experience that hypnotherapy, supported with at least some of the other suggestions in this book, will give you the quickest and most effective relief from anxiety.

You can try a number of other things for a couple of weeks without using hypnotherapy and see how you are doing, maybe you are one of the lucky few whose anxiety does not stem mainly from issues in your subconscious. If you are one of those few, I am very happy for you! But the reality is that most anxiety sufferers have a combination of subconscious issues along with a number of other issues listed in this book.

You may have purchased this book as part of my complete program that already has all of the hypnotherapy recordings for you to listen to. If that is the case, you simply need to read the hypnotherapy companion booklet before you begin to listen to the recordings.

If you purchased this book alone, you can still gain access to the full program and obtain the hypnotherapy recordings that are specifically designed for anxiety and for use with this book. The web address will be listed at the end of this section.

Of course, you can always use another hypnotherapist for hypnosis sessions if you wish. My only caution to you about that is this... not all hypnotherapists are alike. If you choose to use a local hypnotherapist, or an online hypnotherapist, or even someone else's recordings... you cannot necessarily be certain that the person is qualified to work with your anxiety. Do they specialize in anxiety like I do? What type of hypnosis do they typically employ? As you read in the chapter about hypnosis, there are many different hypnotherapy methods and modalities. Some work better for anxiety than others.

Finding the right hypnotherapist for anxiety isn't as simple as it might seem. I am not trying to say that there aren't other hypnotherapists in the world that can work well with anxiety issues... I am simply saying that there are hypnotherapists that are not as qualified to work with anxiety, in my opinion.

I've spoken to people who have seen a hypnotherapist in the past for anxiety, who have felt they received no benefit from the hypnosis. My response to them was that they didn't have the right hypnotherapist. It's just like many other professions, where it's often better to find a specialist than a general practitioner. You wouldn't want your general medical practitioner to perform open heart surgery on you, would you? I specialize in anxiety and phobias.

But I digress.

I'd simply like to say that you *can* get rid of your anxiety, you do not have to live with it and "manage" it the rest of your life. You can get rid of it and you can keep it away or at the very least you can drastically reduce it. I did, and so can you!

To obtain the complete "Be Anxiety Free... Now!" program, visit my website at:

www.beanxietyfreenow.com .

To obtain the complete "Be Anxiety Free...
Now!" program, visit my website at:

www.beanxietyfreenow.com .